Humble King to Conquering King

The Week That Changed Everything

Kurt Litwiller

*Live in the victory
Jesus provided
for you!*
Kurt

Copyright © 2011 by Kurt Litwiller

All rights reserved. No part of this book may be used, reproduced, stored in a retrieval system, or transmitted in any form whatsoever — including electronic, photocopy, recording — without prior written permission from the author, except in the case of brief quotations embodied in critical articles or reviews.

All Scripture quotations, unless otherwise indicated, are taken from the *Holy Bible, New International Version*®. *NIV*®. Copyright © 1973, 1978, 1984 by International Bible Society. Used by permission of Zondervan. All rights reserved.

Edited by Michael Milligan and Carol Cain

FIRST EDITION

ISBN: 9780982947692

Library of Congress Control Number: 2011923506

Published by
NewBookPublishing.com, a division of Reliance Media, Inc.
2395 Apopka Blvd., #200, Apopka, FL 32703
NewBookPublishing.com

Printed in the United States of America

DEDICATION

I dedicate this book to the King of Kings—to the only King who could conquer death and give me eternal life. I view all life through the empty tomb. I realize there are no problems, powers, or plans that can overtake me because I stand with the King. Thank you, Jesus, for providing the way into Your eternal presence! Let my life be pleasing in Your sight, O God, my King. May You receive the glory for this book!

TABLE OF CONTENTS

INTRODUCTION 7

PART 1 THE COMING KING 11
   Triumphant Entry 13
   Woman Anointed Jesus' Feet 23
   The King Will Establish His Kingdom 35
   The Guests Of The King 47

PART 2 THE SACRIFICIAL KING 57
   The Lord's Supper 59
   Remain In Me 69
   Prayers Of Jesus 81
   Jesus' Arrest 91
   Peter's Denials 101
   The Trial 111
   The Cross 123

PART 3 THE RISEN KING 135
   The Empty Tomb 137
   Releasing The Guilt 153
   Road To Emmaus 163
   Thomas' Unbelief 175
   Reminded Of The Gospel 183
   Serve The King 193

CONCLUSION 203

INTRODUCTION

Have you ever looked back at your life and noticed that one decision affected the direction of your entire life? If we think hard enough, most of us are able to point back to different situations that dramatically changed our lives. Whether that was by getting married, losing a job, deciding to go back to school, hearing a dreaded report from the doctor, or losing a child in an accident, we have all had situations that changed the course of our lives.

You may be able to point back to one week when you were frustrated at your dead end job, and you decided to go back to school. In doing so, you found a much better job that took you to a new part of the country, where you found your spouse and raised a family. The decision of one week changed your life dramatically and put you on the course that you are on now.

The decisions that you made in the week may have impacted many other people as well. Think about how you may have altered other people's lives by the choices that you made. Your spouse would not have met you, and they would have married someone else. Your kids would have never been born. Your life would have been so much different if you would have made different decisions in that one week. That week affected everything else and everyone else in your life.

Well, Jesus had one of those weeks. It is the week the church calls "Holy Week." Jesus did not just make another trip to the Holy City of Jerusalem, but it was 'the' trip He was born for. He came to lay down His life to save us from our sins, and then to be raised from the dead to give us power over death. What Jesus did in this one week did not affect a few people here and there, but affected every single person who has ever lived! This week influences not only the rest of our lives here on earth, but the rest of our eternity. Jesus could have called it quits at anytime during that week. At any point He could have called to His Father, and in an instant, He would have been saved from the horrors that he faced.[1] But He endured the entire week for you and for me, and by doing so, He changed everything!

At the beginning of the week, Jesus was a humble king. Jesus had humble beginnings. Even though He was the center of all praise in heaven, He came down as a helpless baby in a feed trough for animals. In His ministry we see that He denied himself the things that were rightfully His. He set aside His glory in heaven and His palace in heaven and roamed the earth with no house to call His own. He was a king, but had no particular plot of land that marked His territory. This king did not have any possessions and did not even have a house to call his own.[2]

However, by week's end, we see Jesus as the conquering King. He is the King above all Kings. He defeats the last enemy, the enemy whom no other king could beat. That enemy is death.[3]

Take this journey with me as we remember this week that changed everything. There are so many benefits that we have received because Jesus was willing to suffer the pain that belonged to us. We no longer have to carry around our sin, our shame, our pain. When He became the conquering King, we His people, shared in the victory!

Humble King To Conquering King

PART 1

THE COMING KING

Rejoice greatly, O Daughter of Zion! Shout, Daughter of Jerusalem! See your king comes to you, righteous and having salvation, gentle and riding on a donkey, on a colt, the foal of a donkey.
                              Zechariah 9:9

Triumphant Entry

What makes a great king? Once there was a King of a large kingdom, and he was growing very old. He decided that it was time to select an heir from among his four sons, so he called them in one at a time to discuss the inheritance of his kingdom. As each son came in, the King said to him, "My son, I am very old and will not live much longer. I wish to entrust my kingdom to the son best suited to receive it. Tell me, if I leave my kingdom to you what will you give to the kingdom?

The first son was very handsome. So he replied, "The kingdom will be drawn to me, because I look like a leader. I look like someone people will want to follow." By his appearance he had all the other sons beat, and that was why he believed that he should become king.

The second son was very rich. He replied, "I am a man of vast wealth. If you leave me the kingdom I will give it my wealth, and it will be the richest kingdom in the world."

The third son was physically strong, so he replied, "I am a man of great strength. If you leave me your kingdom I will give it all of my strength, and it will be the strongest kingdom in the world. People will not be scared to go into battle with me."

The fourth son was not handsome, rich, or strong—it seemed he had nothing to offer. He said, "Father, you know that my brothers are richer, stronger, and more handsome than me. They have spent a lot of time gaining these attributes, while I have spent time among the people in your kingdom. I have shared with them in their sickness and sorrow. And I have learned to love them. I am afraid that the only thing that I have to give to your kingdom is my love for the people. I know that my brothers have more to offer than I do, therefore I will not be disappointed when one of them is named your heir. I will simply go on doing what I have always done."

The time came when the king died and the people anxiously awaited the news of who their new king would be. And the greatest rejoicing the kingdom ever knew took place when the fourth son—the one that took time with the people and loved them—was named king.[4]

This story tells us the greatest attribute of a king is love for his followers. Not looks, strength or riches. Jesus is like the fourth son in this story—He did not have riches…He was poor and had no place to lay his head.[5] He was not strong… He took on frail humanity and people were not drawn to Him because He looked like a warrior. He was not handsome… He had no beauty or majesty to attract us to Him, nothing in His appearance that we should desire Him.[6] Yet this humble King, Jesus, loved the people enough that He shared in their sorrow and pain. He left the splendor of heaven for the pain of this sinful world. What king would leave his palace and all his glory and live in poverty with his subjects? King Jesus would be the only one!

When Jesus was 33 years old, in His third year of His ministry, He came to Jerusalem like He had done a hundred times before. But this time it was different. He came on a simple donkey, and He came to defeat the enemy that opposed us. Luke 19 shows our King riding into the battle on our behalf.

> [28] *After Jesus had said this, he went on ahead, going up to Jerusalem.* [29] *As he approached Bethphage and Bethany at the hill called the Mount of Olives, he sent two of his disciples, saying to them,* [30] *"Go to the village ahead of you, and as you enter it, you will find a colt tied there, which no one has ever ridden. Untie it and bring it here.* [31] *If anyone asks you, 'Why are you untying it?' tell him, 'The Lord needs it.'"*
>
> [32] *Those who were sent ahead went and found it just as he had told them.* [33] *As they were untying the colt, its owners asked them, "Why are you untying the colt?"*
>
> [34] *They replied, "The Lord needs it."*
>
> [35] *They brought it to Jesus, threw their cloaks on the colt and put Jesus on it.* [36] *As he went along, people spread their cloaks on the road.*
>
> [37] *When he came near the place where the road goes down the Mount of Olives, the whole crowd of disciples began joyfully to*

praise God in loud voices for all the miracles they had seen:

[38] *"Blessed is the king who comes in the name of the Lord!"*

"Peace in heaven and glory in the highest!"

[39] *Some of the Pharisees in the crowd said to Jesus, "Teacher, rebuke your disciples!"*

[40] *"I tell you," he replied, "if they keep quiet, the stones will cry out."*

[41] *As he approached Jerusalem and saw the city, he wept over it* [42] *and said, "If you, even you, had only known on this day what would bring you peace—but now it is hidden from your eyes.* [43] *The days will come upon you when your enemies will build an embankment against you and encircle you and hem you in on every side.* [44] *They will dash you to the ground, you and the children within your walls. They will not leave one stone on another, because you did not recognize the time of God's coming to you."*

A King Riding Into Town

This story is mentioned in all four gospels. It is an important story that all four authors wanted us to know. What a sight this must have been. I would have loved to have been in the crowd that day. The crowd welcoming a King! It was during the biggest week of the year at Jerusalem. People came from all over the country to celebrate the Passover in Jerusalem, which is a week-long festival that was held each year. Jerusalem would double in size during the Passover because everyone wanted to be in this Holy City during this holy time. There were so many people in Jerusalem that they could not hold everybody inside the city. There were people camping all over the countryside. Verse 37 says, *"When he came near the place where the road goes down the Mount of Olives the whole crowd of disciples began joyfully to praise God in loud voices for all the miracles they had seen."* And verse 41 starts off saying, *"As he approached Jerusalem..."* Jesus was not even to Jerusalem yet. He was well outside the city gates when people gathered around Him and started to praise their King. The people were lining the street to prepare the way for Him to get to Jerusalem. This crowd knew Jesus was special. They gave Him the red carpet treatment. They laid down their cloaks on the ground so that He could ride over them. They sensed that Jesus was royalty.

One of the gospels says that the people came out to meet Jesus and were waving palm branches. John 12:13 says, *"They took palm branches and went out to meet him, shouting, Hosanna! Blessed is he who comes in the name of the Lord! Blessed is the King of Israel!"* This action had a special meaning. After war, people would run out and meet their victorious king by waving palm branches. Palm branches were used in victory celebrations. We get this same image in Revelation 7:9. It says, *"After this I looked and there before me was a great multitude that no one could count, from every nation, tribe, people and language, standing before the* throne and in front of the Lamb. They were wearing white robes and were holding palm branches in their hands." They are before the throne holding palm branches…symbolizing victory. God had won the fight and they are celebrating with their victorious King around the throne. So in this passage, as Jesus comes towards Jerusalem and they come out with their palm branches—that is the people's way of saying that Jesus is a <u>victorious</u> <u>King</u>.

If Jesus is a king you would think that He would be riding a horse…a king's horse, not a donkey. He could have displayed more power riding a strong horse into town, just like He had won a battle. But Jesus made His directions clear to His disciples in verse 30-31, *"Go to the village ahead of you, and as you enter it, you will find a colt tied there, which no one has ever ridden. Untie it and bring it here. If anyone asks you, why are you untying it? Tell him, the Lord needs it."* Jesus did not say, "bring me…let's see…either a horse, donkey, or camel. Just give me something that I can ride into Jerusalem." Jesus said to bring Him a colt. Very specific! Jesus walked everywhere He went…why now, when He is only a couple of miles away from Jerusalem does He want to ride a donkey? He must have been really tired if He couldn't walk a couple more miles. Why didn't He walk, or why didn't He ride a king's horse into Jerusalem? Our answer is found in the Old Testament. Zechariah 9:9, *"Rejoice greatly, O Daughter of Zion! Shout, Daughter of Jerusalem! See your king comes to you, righteous and having salvation, gentle and riding on a donkey, on a colt, the foal of a donkey."* This is a prediction that was made hundreds of years earlier—that a king would come to Jerusalem, bringing righteousness and salvation, and he would come on a donkey. I love to read the Bible and see how it all fits together. It is no accident how things worked out that day. It wasn't like Jesus rode into Jerusalem and thought, "Oh neat, I guess I just fulfilled another prophecy." God had this all planned out the entire time—a king would come riding into Jerusalem on a donkey.

We Need To Choose: Worship Or Reject Him

This passage is one big praise gathering. There were shouts of praise, songs of joy, laughing, hearts full of gratitude. I can see people dancing and having a good time. It says they were praising God for all of the miracles that He had done. Jesus' ministry was full of miracles and people's lives were dramatically affected by Him. Jesus healed the lepers, the blind, the deaf and the demon possessed; He turned water into wine; He fed the 5000 with five loaves of bread and two fish; and He raised Lazarus from the dead. And because of all this, the people came to bring their praises to their King. Much like these people, we should find ourselves wanting to praise Him for all of the things that He has done for us. But some in the crowd didn't like what they saw. The Pharisees were angry that the crowd was exalting Jesus. Verse 39 says, *"Some of the Pharisees in the crowd came to Jesus, 'Teacher, rebuke your disciples!'"* The Pharisees wanted Jesus to rebuke His disciples. They were saying, "Jesus, your disciples are doing something wrong! They are exalting you as king. You are not a king. So stop them!" I love Jesus' response here in verse

40, *"'I tell you,' he replied, 'if they keep quiet, the stones will cry out.'"* If people stop praising God, the stones will do it. Creation will praise God in their place.

If you were in the crowd that day and a Pharisee asked you to stop praising God, would you have? Is there anything or anybody that keeps you from giving God the praise that He deserves? We read in this passage how the crowd is praising its King, but how quickly they switch their attitudes. Less than a week later this crowd in Jerusalem is not screaming out songs of joy anymore, but they are screaming out curses. It was the crowd that determined Jesus' death. Pilate asked the crowd to choose who they wanted to crucify. The crowd was swayed by the religious rulers and they asked for Jesus to be crucified. When they were with Jesus' disciples they joined in the praises. "Our King is here." And when they were with another group of people, "King…He is no king. Kill Him." Are we guilty of any of that in our lives? When we are around our Christian brothers and sisters and we are free with our expressions we may exclaim, "King Jesus we praise you." But when we get around other people who think differently, we become different ourselves. By our actions and words we say, "Jesus—King, I never gave it much thought."

This crowd changed their tune on a dime. This is not the political Messiah that they were hoping for, so they had doubts in their minds. Then the Pharisees came along and turned them against Jesus. The crowd didn't believe in Jesus strongly enough, and they were swayed by the people they hung around with. That is something for us to be aware of. Monitor your behavior when you are with different sets of people. See if you praise God with one group and turn your back on Him with another group. There may be some people reading this who worship Him on Sunday, get lost in the worship and the Word, but during the week when they are under the pressures of the world—have a completely different outlook on God. Make sure you praise your King, no matter who you are around!

What is interesting about this passage is…we have just seen a huge celebration, a praise gathering, and at the end…Jesus is weeping. Not a tear in His eye, but weeping over Jerusalem. Why is He crying? This should be the best moment of His life. The people just came to the decision that He is King. Usually when a king is announced it is a happy occasion. But Jesus knew what was ahead. He knew that they would reject Him as the king. He saw that their rejection of His kingship would bring great judgment upon them. Verse 41-44 says, *"As he approached Jerusalem and saw the city, he wept over it and said, If you, even you, had only known on this day what would bring you peace—but now it is hidden from your eyes. The days will come upon you when your enemies will build an embankment against you and encircle you and hem you in on every side. They will dash you to the ground, you and the children within your walls. They will not leave one stone on another, because you did not recognize the time of God's coming to you."* Jerusalem's rejection of Jesus cost them dearly. Jerusalem fell, people were killed, the temple completely destroyed. And that happened in 70AD. Jesus is mourning for the future of the people of Jerusalem.

This passage starts out full of praise and ends with

one of the saddest verses of the Bible. The last sentence of this passage says, *"They will not leave one stone on another, because you did not recognize the time of God's coming to you."* Destruction happened to them because they didn't recognize God's coming to them. THEY MISSED THEIR KING!! It is the same way for us today as individuals. Destruction is going to come to us, if we don't recognize God's coming to us. Don't miss your King!

God is here with us today, He wants to embrace you as one of His people. The Pharisees were too prideful to see God's coming to them in Jesus Christ. They wouldn't open up their eyes to see Him. If you don't know Jesus Christ as Lord and Savior, open up your eyes and see that God is coming to you right now. Don't go to sleep tonight blind to the fact God is coming to you, because just like Jerusalem, you won't like the results.

King Jesus came according to Zechariah 9:9 to bring salvation. He gives us eternal life by washing away our sins through the sacrifice of the cross. Salvation is available to all of us today. You can reject it, or stand up and praise Him as your King. Praise Him for the salvation He brings!

WOMAN ANOINTED JESUS' FEET

A four year old boy named Jimmy was thrilled when his family got a piano. Immediately he was up on the piano bench pounding on the keys. After a while he climbed down in frustration. "It's no use!" he said. "Jesus Loves Me' just isn't in there!" Moral of the story: You get out, what you put into it![7] The problem he ran into was that he didn't take the time to practice and learn the song. If he put in the time, he would be able to play the song beautifully. But he wanted the song without putting in the practice.

The same thing could be said about our relationship with God. We want all the benefits of God, but we would rather not invest ourselves to get it. If you don't take the time to sit at His feet and praise Him and learn about Him…how can you expect to have a close relationship with Him? You can't know His love, and you can't sense His peace unless you truly know the One who gives it. Mark 14 gives us a story of a woman who was desperate to worship her King.

[1] Now the Passover and the Feast of Unleavened Bread were only two days away, and the chief priests and the teachers of the

law were looking for some sly way to arrest Jesus and kill him. [2] "But not during the Feast," they said, "or the people may riot."

[3] While he was in Bethany, reclining at the table in the home of a man known as Simon the Leper, a woman came with an alabaster jar of very expensive perfume, made of pure nard. She broke the jar and poured the perfume on his head.

[4] Some of those present were saying indignantly to one another, "Why this waste of perfume? [5] It could have been sold for more than a year's wages and the money given to the poor." And they rebuked her harshly.

[6] "Leave her alone," said Jesus. "Why are you bothering her? She has done a beautiful thing to me. [7] The poor you will always have with you, and you can help them any time you want. But you will not always have me. [8] She did what she could. She poured perfume on my body beforehand to prepare for my burial. [9] I tell you the truth, wherever the gospel is preached throughout the world, what she has done will also be told, in memory of her."

[10] Then Judas Iscariot, one of the Twelve, went to the chief priests to betray Jesus to them. [11] They were delighted to hear this and promised to give him money. So he watched for an opportunity to hand him over.

Costly Worship

Our desire for God comes about because we see our need for Him. If we don't see a need for God in our lives, we will not have a passion to worship Him. Worship is a natural response once we see all that Jesus has done for us. In this passage, this woman obviously saw her need for Jesus. She wouldn't have acted like this for just anybody who came along.

Mark does not tell us this woman's name, but the gospel of John tells us that it is Mary. Mary is the sister of Martha and Lazarus. Lazarus was the person who Jesus raised from the dead. A closer look at Mary reveals a lot about her. She is mentioned three times in the Bible. It is interesting to see what she was doing each time. In Luke 10:38-42, Jesus was at her house and her sister Martha was preparing the meal, while Mary sat at Jesus feet listening to Him. In John 11:31-32, Mary's brother Lazarus had died, and Mary ran out and fell at His feet. And in John 12:1-8, a parallel passage to this one—Mary fell to the ground and poured perfume on Jesus feet and wiped them with her hair. Each time Mary is mentioned in the Bible, she is down on the ground at the feet of Jesus. Mary desires to sit at Jesus' feet.

It is customary to anoint the heads of important guests, but Mary's action was extreme. This was not a $25 jar of perfume that you buy at Macy's, this is the best perfume that you can find. Verse 3 tells us that it was pure nard. It was pure, it wasn't watered down to last longer, and she didn't use a second rate material. Mark tells us the cost of this perfume was over a year's wages. Think about how much that would be today. Would you be willing to give up a year's wages? You may say, if I had a lot of money I would love to give that to Jesus. But look closely at this woman. She is not a millionaire. She was not giving out of her wealth; she was giving out of her love. The beginning of verse 8 says, *"She did what she could."* Literally, this means, "What she had she did." In other words, she gave all she could. She didn't have another five jars of perfume at home. She brought what she had and sacrificed it for Jesus. The woman knew there was no better use for this perfume than to honor Jesus with it.

When we come before Jesus—do we bring our all—or do we just bring a token sacrifice of praise? It was a significant sacrifice for her, but there is no doubt that it was worth it. It demonstrated the feelings that she had in her heart for Jesus. She was not walking away from this incident thinking, "should I have done this or not?" She went away knowing that she laid out her heart before Jesus.

Sometimes worship is costly. This story reminds me of another woman in the Bible. People would go to the temple and drop large amounts of money into the treasury, but an old widow woman dropped in two small coins.[8] Jesus said that she gave more than all of the rest because she gave all she had. Both women serve as examples of total commitment. They are people who held nothing back. There is something about costly worship. King David is another example. Someone offered to give him an oxen to sacrifice to God since he was the king. But King David said in 2 Samuel 24:24, *"No I insist on paying you for it. I will not sacrifice to the Lord my God burnt offerings that cost me nothing."* David says, I want it to be from me, it is not my worship unless it cost me something. Worship is costly.

In this Mark 14 passage: Mary, being a woman, would not have been very influential. People were sure to scoff at what she was doing. But she didn't care what people thought about her. She had one thing on her mind, and that was to worship Jesus. I imagine Mary could have come up with a hundred different excuses why she shouldn't go and worship Jesus. They won't welcome me. They will laugh at me. I have other things that are pressing today that I need to do. I don't want to give up this much to worship Him. But she went, and her worship was treasured by Jesus. I wonder how often we have second thoughts about worshiping Jesus? I am pretty busy, I have a lot of things going on. If I go to worship today, I will have to sacrifice too much. There are other things that I would rather do today.

Too often we decide for one reason or another, not to worship Him. And oh how we miss out when we choose not to worship. We miss out on that special encounter with Jesus. Mary will never forget that day when she poured perfume on Jesus' feet. In a public place with many people around, it was an intimate time of worship that she had with Jesus. Much like when we go to church with a sanctuary full of people standing around us…yet we can encounter Jesus in a very personal intimate way.

I have always wondered what Jesus' reaction was as Mary was worshiping Him. His heart was probably moved and beaming with joy, His eyes full of love for this child of

His who was showing this sacrificial worship. How do you think God is looking at you as you pour out your heart in worship before Him today? If your heart is pure and you are truly seeking Him…I imagine He looks at you as He looked at Mary. In verse 6 Jesus says, *"You have done a beautiful thing to me."* I can't help but believe that He treasures our worship, that our worship is a beautiful thing to Him.

Criticizing Worship

The worship that Mary offered was costly, while other people criticized her for it. People were muttering in the background, "She shouldn't be doing this." Those who were there saw this beautiful thing being done to Jesus and all that they could do was think about all of the money that they could have received for the perfume. They criticized her worship. They could not understand what she was doing— they didn't feel compelled to do the same thing—so they thought it had to be wrong. Their objection was that all of the perfume could be sold and the money given to the poor. The Old Testament does say many times that we are to take care of the poor in the land. I am sure that Jesus wouldn't have had a problem with Mary selling the perfume and giving it to the poor. But what He did have a problem with was the people telling her that her choice of worship was wrong.

We shouldn't stop worshiping God because we are afraid of what people will say. The opposite is also true. We shouldn't stand back and judge or criticize others as they are worshiping as they see fit. Too often we look at what other people are doing, instead of focusing on what we should be doing. The people in the crowd could have brought perfume or money—but they didn't. And they criticized the one who did. I can hear them as the perfume is being poured upon Jesus head, "What a waste of perfume"…as they keep their perfume for a much nobler cause! We can't be critical of other people's worship to God.

> One day a disciple said to his pastor: "Pastor, my six brothers are asleep and I alone have remained awake to worship God." The Pastor answered, "It would have been better for you to remain asleep, if your worship of God is to be mixed with accusations against your brothers."[9]

We do not have a heart of worship when we are tearing other people down. Too often we judge the worship services. "Today was a good one," or "today I didn't get anything out of the service." "I wish we wouldn't worship in this way, it will be more beneficial to worship that way." "We need to sing more hymns," or "we need to sing more praise songs." Worship is the expression of praise to the Lord, an overflow of the heart in praise. I can worship God with hymns, I can worship God with praise songs, and dare I say it: I can even worship God without any music at all. Many times worship becomes all about me. ME, ME, ME. This is what I want! But true worship has nothing to do with me, it is an emptying of myself, and it is all about God. Like the song <u>Heart of Worship</u> says, "I'm coming back to the heart of worship, and it's all about You, all about You Jesus." Mary's focus was completely on Jesus, she was not giving any thought to herself. Mary was so devoted to Jesus that she didn't care what other people thought of her worship. "What will people think if I go in there and do this extreme act of devotion? I don't want people to think I am weird." She didn't care if Judas or other people were over there laughing at her or thinking poorly of her. "If they don't want to worship, that is their problem. I need to show my love to Jesus."

Another example of someone not concerned with what people thought of him as he worshiped the Lord was David in the Old Testament. When the Ark of the Covenant was brought back to Jerusalem after being in enemy hands, it was a great day. The Bible says David went before the ark and was dancing with all his might.[10] David's wife was watching from the window and told David later that it was inappropriate for him as a king to dance that way in front of the servant girls. David's response, "I will become even more undignified than this." He was going to show his joy to the Lord no matter what anyone else thought.

Do we worry about what other people think of our worship? What will other people think if I raise my hands in worship? What will people think if I shout out AMEN during the sermon? Would people look at me strangely if at some point during the service I fell to my knees before the Lord? Worship is putting our focus upon Jesus and responding accordingly—no matter if others criticize or critique what you do. I don't care if it is in the middle of a song or during the sermon, if the Lord stirs you to raise your hand, or get on your knees, do it. Mary wasn't embarrassed to get on her knees in worship in front of a bunch of people, and we shouldn't be either. There will always be someone who thinks your worship is wrong or inappropriate. Will you only worship when other people approve?

One person in particular who did not approve of Mary's worship was Judas Iscariot. Judas is the opposite of Mary. Mary shows desire to worship Jesus, while Judas' only concern was financial gain. Verses 10-11 says, *"Then Judas Iscariot, one of the Twelve, went to the chief priests to betray Jesus to them. They were delighted to hear this and promised to give Him money. So he watched for an opportunity to hand him over."* Can you see the difference in attitude between Judas and Mary? Mary pours a year's worth of wages of perfume on Jesus to worship Him (to show her love)—while Judas turns his back upon Jesus and hands Him over to be killed for four months' wages (30 pieces of silver). Judas is willing to sacrifice Jesus to obtain material gain for himself, while Mary is willing to sacrifice material things to worship Jesus. Their actions revealed the condition of their hearts. Her heart was full of gratitude to God, which led to an extravagant action, while Judas' heart was full of selfishness, which led to betrayal. John 12:6 shows Judas' motives. *"He (Judas) did not say this because he cared about the poor but because he was a thief; as keeper of the money bag, he used to help himself to what was put into it."* Judas followed Jesus for three years. He saw all of the miracles that Jesus performed. He saw the blind receive their sight; he saw the deaf gain their hearing; and he saw Jesus raise the dead. He saw some incredible things. He heard the teachings of Jesus, yet somewhere along the line he decided that he cared more about the things of the world. There may be some people reading this that are like Judas. They may go to church on a regular basis, hear Jesus' teachings often, and see great things happen in the church…but their loyalty is not to Jesus, but to the world. There is a significant warning that we all need to hear over and over again: <u>a knowledge of Jesus and who He is will not save us</u>. Just ask Judas; he knew Jesus very well. It is about living our lives in response to the grace that He gave us.

I find it interesting that as you step back and look at this entire Mark 14 passage, you can see a contrast in how people react to Jesus. In verse 1 we see that the religious people wanted Jesus dead. And we see at the very end of the passage, that one of the disciples, Judas Iscariot, was willing to hand Jesus over to be crucified. In between these two examples of rejection of Jesus, is a beautiful story. A story of a woman who gives everything she has to worship her Lord. And you can see this same story played out in our world today. We live in a world where we are surrounded by people who want the thought of Jesus to be dead; they don't want to talk about Him. "Let's get rid of anything that has to do with Jesus." And there are others who claim to follow God, but in the end they are more like Judas. They are concerned with their own lives and their own prosperity on this earth. In the midst of all this, we see other people bringing radical worship to the Lord—a radical worship that doesn't make sense to those who are perishing. But to us who are being saved, it is just a response to the overwhelming feeling that we have inside. Worship your king, no matter what other people think of you. Your worship is between you and the King!

THE KING WILL ESTABLISH HIS KINGDOM

Europe's biggest lottery ever stood at 66 million Euros (which is equivalent to about 90 million U.S. dollars). Without a winner, the jackpot rolled over for six months. The amount was too much for an Italian man not to give it a try—so he purchased a ticket. On the day the winning lottery numbers were revealed, the man was preoccupied with the details of a huge project at work. In the midst of his busy schedule, the man forgot to find out the winning number. By the time he realized he had the winning ticket, the deadline for claiming the jackpot of a lifetime had passed. He missed out on a huge treasure![11]

Just think of having something that valuable at your disposal and not cashing in on it. We all have the winning ticket in Jesus, the most valuable prize imaginable, yet so many people don't claim the prize. Jesus says that not everyone who voices out "Lord, Lord" will be saved.[12] You actually have to follow through and cash in the ticket by submitting your life to Jesus' Lordship. Jesus is going to return and physically set up His kingdom. There is no doubt about it. This humble King shares about the coming of His kingdom in Matthew 24.

> [36] "No one knows about that day or hour, not even the angels in heaven, nor the Son, but only the Father. [37] As it was in the days of Noah, so it will be at the coming of the Son of Man. [38] For in the days before the flood, people were eating and drinking, marrying and giving in marriage, up to the day Noah entered the ark; [39] and they knew nothing about what would happen until the flood came and took them all away. That is how it will be at the coming of the Son of Man. [40] Two men will be in the field; one will be taken and the other left. [41] Two women will be grinding with a hand mill; one will be taken and the other left.
>
> [42] "Therefore keep watch, because you do not know on what day your Lord will come. [43] But understand this: If the owner of the house had known at what time of night the thief was coming, he would have kept watch and would not have let his house be broken into. [44] So you also must be ready, because the Son of Man will come at an hour when you do not expect him.
>
> [45] "Who then is the faithful and wise servant, whom the master has put in charge of the

servants in his household to give them their food at the proper time? ⁴⁶ It will be good for that servant whose master finds him doing so when he returns. ⁴⁷ I tell you the truth, he will put him in charge of all his possessions. ⁴⁸ But suppose that servant is wicked and says to himself, 'My master is staying away a long time,' ⁴⁹ and he then begins to beat his fellow servants and to eat and drink with drunkards. ⁵⁰ The master of that servant will come on a day when he does not expect him and at an hour he is not aware of. ⁵¹ He will cut him to pieces and assign him a place with the hypocrites, where there will be weeping and gnashing of teeth.

As Jesus was on the earth revealing God's first coming to man, He taught about His second coming. There were many people who missed God's first coming and they paid dearly. We saw in chapter 1 that their rejection of God during His first coming brought destruction on them, on Jerusalem, and on the temple. Jesus warns us in this passage, "Be sure you are ready for my second coming." We see that there are severe consequences for those who are not ready.

Jesus has promised us that He is going to come back. But He never gave us a definite time. He didn't say that He would be back on any certain day or even a certain year. In fact, in this passage Jesus says that He doesn't even know when He will come back. Verse 36 says, *"No one knows about that day or hour, not even the angels in heaven, nor the Son, but only the Father."* There are a lot of people that have tried to predict Jesus' coming. To this point, they have obviously all been wrong. And they will continue to be wrong because there is no way that they can know. We don't know if Jesus will come back today, tomorrow, next week, or 300 years from now. One of my favorite sayings is, "God's coming is just around the block, but we don't know how long His block is." It could happen at any time. He may come in the morning, night or noontime. We don't know when it will be, so Jesus tells us to be ready at all times. Jesus says that if a man knew when his house was going to be robbed, he would keep watch and stop the robber. If we knew when Jesus was coming back, we could wait till the day before to get right with Him. But we don't know. We may die before He comes back. I've seen a bumper sticker on a car that says something like this, "People who plan to seek God at the 11th hour, die at 10:30." Now is the time to seek Him because tomorrow may be too late.

    We need to be ready at all times because Jesus is going to come whether we are ready or not. It's like playing hide and seek. One person counts and when he is done counting, he says, "ready or not—here I come." If you're not ready, that is too bad...you just lost. You're going to be easy to find. We need to be ready for Jesus' final countdown to His return because when He says ready or not here I come...if we are not ready, we are the big losers. Verse 50-51 says, *"The master of that servant will come on a day when he does not expect him and at an hour he is not aware of. He will cut him to pieces and assign him a place with the hypocrites, where there will be weeping and gnashing of teeth."* Hear that! He will cut him to pieces and assign him a place where there will be weeping and gnashing of teeth. It will not be pleasant for those who are not prepared—for those who take His return lightly will be faced with eternal punishment. The Bible talks a lot about hell. It is a real place. It says it is a place where the fire never goes out and the worm never dies. It is a place of torment, of weeping and gnashing of teeth. A place separated from God. It is assigned to those who are not ready for Christ's return. But for us who are right with the Lord and have surrendered our lives to Him, we can look forward to an eternity of bliss. No more pain, no more sorrow, no more mourning, or crying, no more death. We will be in His presence forever. But this place is reserved for those who Jesus finds doing His work when He returns. Are you the servant that is working for your master while He is gone?

If He came back today, would He find you doing His work? Or would He find you doing something for yourself? I am happy to go about my master's business—no one has to try to talk me into doing things for God. I want to. I do the work He has assigned for me because I love Him. And when He comes back I want to hear Him say, "Well done my good and faithful servant. Come and share your master's happiness." Well done. You did the work I wanted you to do. I am proud of you. I don't want to be the servant who gets lackadaisical because my master has been gone a long time. We need to live each day with urgency. There is a quote that says, "I am going to live like Jesus died yesterday, rose today, and is coming back tomorrow." We need to live each moment as if Jesus were coming back right now. Would I want Him to hear me yelling at my coworker or gossiping to one of my friends? Would I want Him to come back as I am looking at something bad on the internet or on TV? I would rather Him come back while I'm living a life committed to Him. I hope He returns and finds me about His work: treating people with love, going out of my way to help people, bringing peace to relationships. I hope He comes back and finds me reading His Word, praying, building up His kingdom.

Sometimes we may find it hard to live with urgency because Jesus hasn't been here in 2000 years. It has been a long time—and it always feels like Jesus is not coming back today. We have a tendency to lose our focus. But Jesus says in verse 46, *"It will be good for that servant whose master finds him doing so when he returns."* It will be good for us doing our master's work when He returns. Matthew chapters 24-25 both have to do with Jesus' return. I encourage you to read these two chapters. There is a parable in Matthew 25 of the sheep and the goats. At the end of the age, God is going to separate us: Those for eternal life and those for eternal punishment. Jesus says in the parable, *"Whatever you do for the least of these, you do for me."* And *"And whatever you didn't do for the least of these, you didn't do for me."* Have you ever thought about that? It should make us treat people differently. When you gossip about someone or put them down, it is like you are putting down Jesus. When you cheat someone, it is like you are cheating Jesus. When you feed someone who is hungry, it is like you are feeding Jesus.

How we treat other people is a heart issue…so in the same way it is like we are doing it to Jesus. When He comes back will He find us practicing compassion towards one another?

When He comes—He is not going to ask you how big your house was, or what kind of car you drove. He will not ask you what your job title was. He won't be concerned with the fancy suits or dresses in your closet. He's more concerned with how you helped others and shared His name with those who needed to hear it.

The Bible makes it clear that not everyone will be ready. Back in Matthew 24, verses 40 & 41 Jesus says, *"Two men will be in the field; one will be taken and the other left. Two women will be grinding with a hand mill; one will be taken and the other left."* This passage is not trying to tell us that 50% of the people will be saved (one taken, one left). Jesus tells us plainly that the road to heaven is a narrow road.[13] This verse is just trying to give us a wake-up call that some will not be ready to spend eternity with the Lord. And many of these people are close to one another. They are people who work together. Yet only one of them will be ready for Jesus' return. Luke also shares this same teaching of Jesus. In Luke 17:34 it says, *"I tell you, on that night two people will be in one bed; one will be taken and the other left."* Obviously these two people are close to one another if they are sleeping in the same bed. Yet one is ready and the other is not. Just because your spouse is ready, doesn't mean you are automatically ready. We stand before God individually, not as a couple. It doesn't matter who our parents are or how good our family name is. It doesn't matter who you know. It comes down to whether or not you have followed Jesus and made Him Lord of your life. It is very important to be ready. It is not like when you miss a flight and can get on the next one. There is no other flight to heaven. You must be ready when He returns!

Jesus' Warning

Jesus gives us a little warning about what it will be like if we are not ready. In Luke 17:20-37, He uses two illustrations to get His point across. He talks about Noah and about Sodom. These stories were about two great periods of judgment against humanity. Do you think that people in Noah's day were aware that a flood was coming? No. If they knew about it they would have been like Noah and built a boat to prepare for it. Do you think that people at Sodom knew their destruction was coming on that day? No. They would have left town if they had known the destruction was coming. They didn't prepare for the destruction because they didn't see it coming. They just lived each day like they did the day before with no thought of changing their lifestyles. Luke 17:27-28 says, *"People were eating, drinking, marrying and being given in marriage up to the day Noah entered the ark. Then the flood came and destroyed them all. It was the same in the days of Lot. People were eating and drinking, buying and selling, planting and building. But the day Lot left Sodom, fire and sulfur rained down from heaven and destroyed them all."* One day they were living their lives, the next day they faced the wrath of God. These people were involved in everyday activities. Some of those activities were evil in God's sight, but the ones mentioned here are not wrong. They were being married, they were buying and selling, building and planting. These things are not wrong in themselves. The crime is that people were simply ignoring God. Noah and Lot lived their lives right before God, they were in tune with God, and they were able to escape the judgment that came. I want us to be careful that we, also, don't get so caught up in the buying and selling, and the building and planting. We can't get so caught up in life that we don't take time to seek the Lord and walk in His ways.

Both of these illustrations (Noah and Sodom) show the absolute finality of God's judgment. If you were not in the ark, you died. If you didn't leave Sodom, you died. As the rains came down and as the fire came down from Heaven, it was too late to change your ways. The idea that there is a second chance on judgment day is a myth. Hebrews 9:27 says, *"Just as man is destined to die once, and after that to face judgment."* Sodom had no second chance…people in Noah's day didn't have a second chance on the day of their judgment. They were destroyed because of the lives they choose to live. We have one time around to make the correct decisions, to be in the place of Noah, and not in the place of the people who were swept away in the flood.

In 2005, Hurricane Katrina was one of the biggest disasters to strike the United States. People in New Orleans were warned about the storm and told to evacuate. Very few took the warning seriously. They believed that the storm wouldn't affect them or that it wouldn't be very bad. But over

1,800 people lost their lives. In that same year, Hurricane Rita tore over the Florida Keys to Louisiana and Texas. Before the hurricane the people were told to evacuate. It was reported that a large percentage of people left because they saw what had happened in New Orleans. They left because the same destruction <u>might</u> be on the way. They learned from what happened before, and it was reported that only seven people died as a result of that hurricane. THEY LEARNED FROM WHAT TOOK PLACE IN THE PAST. That is what Jesus is talking about in this passage of scripture. Learn from the past. As Christians we know that destruction is coming upon people who live ungodly lives…we have been warned by scripture and we have seen the examples of judgment in Noah and Sodom…so we should heed the warnings of the judgment to come.

On the day that Jesus comes back, nothing else will matter. All of our possessions will be worthless on that day. Jesus says in Luke 17:31, *"On that day no one who is on the roof of his house, with his goods inside, should go down to get them."* You will not take your possessions with you—why would you want to? When Christ comes back, all of our possessions will be worth nothing and we will have no desire to have them. When you see Jesus break through the Eastern sky in all His glory—you won't have a desire to go back into your house to get your big screen TV and your Wii. It is going to happen in a blink of an eye—and we need to be ready to go at that moment.

Just because someone attends church doesn't mean that they have surrendered their life to the Lord and are ready for His return. We need to live the lives that we sing about on Sunday mornings. Just because we talk about Christ's return doesn't mean we are ready for His return.

> There is a story of burglars who broke into a New York business which manufactures burglar-proof glass. To get in, they smashed a big glass-panel door. They got away with a large amount of merchandise. The president of the firm said, "It never occurred to us, to put our own burglar-proof glass on our door."[14]

They sold the product, but they didn't use it themselves. Just because we claim to be Christians, doesn't make it so. The Apostle Paul says in 1 Corinthians 9:27, *"No, I beat my body and make it my slave so that after I have preached to others, I myself will not be disqualified for the prize."* The apostle Paul, great man of faith that he was, says he doesn't want to preach to others and then be disqualified himself. He beat his body and he disciplined himself to live out that which he preached. He made himself ready for the day he would stand before the Lord face to face. Many people are cheating on God. Could you imagine cheating on your spouse and having them come home and catch you? Now, imagine the lifestyle we lead, and imagine it's the day Jesus returns. Will He find us faithful?

I want to close this chapter with a story that a man shared about a time when he was a boy.

He took a tour of the Henry Ford factory in Dearborn, Michigan. He saw an electro-magnetic crane move over a large railroad car filled with what seemed to be junk steel. At the flip of a switch, everything in that car leaped up to the magnetic crane. Then he saw a strange thing: some pieces fell back into the car. He waited until the others had left and then climbed up to look inside and found out why these pieces fell back in. He found that they were two by fours, a broom handle, and some broken pieces of wood. Only objects made of the right component responded to the magnet; the rest were left behind.[15]

We need to examine our lives to see if they are made of the right component. When Jesus comes back, He is going to call us to meet Him in the air—turn on His magnet so to speak. The people who have hearts that seek after Him, will be called to Him. And those whose hearts are seeking after this world will be left behind. ARE YOU READY?

THE GUESTS OF THE KING

There was a man who got lost in the desert and was about to die of thirst. Luckily he came upon an old, abandoned shack out in the middle of nowhere. No one was around so he decided to take shelter from the hot desert heat. He looked around and saw an old rusty water pump about 15 feet away from the house. He ran out to the pump and he pumped like crazy, but nothing came out. Disappointed, he was about to turn and leave when he saw a jug with a note attached to it. The note said, "You have to prime the pump with all the water in this jug to get water out of the pump. P.S. Make sure you fill the jug before you leave for the next person." The man popped the cork off the top of the jug and it was almost full of water. Suddenly he had a decision to make, would he just drink the water that was there, knowing it was in his hands…or would he have faith and pour the water down the pump to get more. He wrestled with the decision, and finally decided to pour the water into the pump. Then he pumped and pumped; no water was coming out. After a little while the water came flowing out. He had all the water he would ever need. He filled up the jug and left a note for the next guy, "believe me, it really works."[16]

What would you have done in that situation? I imagine there would be some people who would drink what's in the jug, just to make sure they had water to drink. But they would have missed out on all of the water that is available to them, and missed out on the chance to help someone else out as well. We have the same kind of choice in our life. Count on what we see, or have faith that there is abundantly more that we cannot see (heaven). Will you settle for what you can see, sacrificing the things you cannot? Because, just like in this illustration, you have to completely surrender the jug of water before you can have an endless supply of water.

Do we settle for the things of this life because we can see them, touch them, and know that we have them? We have instructions (the Bible) that point us to more. If we give what we have to Him, He will give us unlimited resources that we can't see. Is it hard to come to this point of surrender? Yes, you bet…that is why they call it faith. Let's read Matthew 22:1-14.

> *[1]Jesus spoke to them again in parables, saying: [2] "The kingdom of heaven is like a king who prepared a wedding banquet for his son. [3] He sent his servants to those who had been invited to the banquet to tell them to come, but they refused to come.*
>
> *[4] "Then he sent some more servants and said, 'Tell those who have been invited that I have*

prepared my dinner: My oxen and fattened cattle have been butchered, and everything is ready. Come to the wedding banquet.'

[5] *"But they paid no attention and went off— one to his field, another to his business.* [6] *The rest seized his servants, mistreated them and killed them.* [7] *The king was enraged. He sent his army and destroyed those murderers and burned their city.*

[8] *"Then he said to his servants, 'The wedding banquet is ready, but those I invited did not deserve to come.* [9] *Go to the street corners and invite to the banquet anyone you find.'* [10] *So the servants went out into the streets and gathered all the people they could find, both good and bad, and the wedding hall was filled with guests.*

[11] *"But when the king came in to see the guests, he noticed a man there who was not wearing wedding clothes.* [12] *'Friend,' he asked, 'how did you get in here without wedding clothes?' The man was speechless.*

[13] *"Then the king told the attendants, 'Tie him hand and foot, and throw him outside, into the darkness, where there will be weeping and gnashing of teeth.'*

[14] *"For many are invited, but few are chosen."*

Jesus often speaks to the crowds by using parables. A parable is a story that has spiritual meaning wrapped up inside of it. The crowd could go home entertained, "good story Jesus", or they could really think and search out the meaning that Jesus was teaching them. We have that choice today. Do we truly want to seek out what God is saying? This parable is about a King throwing a wedding banquet for his son. The King is God, and the banquet is for Jesus and His bride. It is a picture of the end of time celebration when Jesus comes back for His bride, the church (the people who believe in Him and who have given their lives to live for Jesus). There are three different reactions to the wedding banquet the king threw for His son.

People Rejected The Invitation

Those who were invited and those who went to the party were two completely different people. The host of the banquet would invite people days, weeks, or months before a banquet would take place—then people would accept or decline the invitation. Then on the day of the banquet the host would send his servants to tell the people who accepted the invitation that the meal is ready. Come. But in this parable, even though the people initially accepted the invitation, they backed out because other things came up.

Luke 14 shares the same wedding banquet story. In this passage the men came up with three different excuses why they couldn't come to the party. The excuses that they gave were really not very good excuses at all. They were just trying to get out of following through with their commitment. The first one says "I have just bought a field, and I must go and see it. Please excuse me." At first glance it seems like a reasonable thing to miss a party for. But who buys a field without looking at it. Would any farmer spend all of that money to buy a field without seeing what it looks like? Is it hilly or flat? Does it have good soil or is it rocky. The second man says "I have just bought five yoke of oxen, and I'm on my way to try them out. Please excuse me." Again to buy oxen without first trying them out is not a probable thing. It is like buying a car without test driving it. You want to try it out to make sure it will perform the way that it should. This man uses this bad excuse to excuse himself from the party. The third man said, "I just got married, so I can't come." The man knew when he accepted the first invitation whether he would be married or not. He now wants to get out of the party so he uses his marriage as an excuse not to go to the party. It is hard to understand their thinking. They accepted the invitation, but now they let little things get in the way of actually going to the party. Even if they did buy a field or oxen, they could have checked it out earlier that day or the next day. Go to the party. Not going to the party would be a great insult to the host who invited you.

    Jesus had a meaning to this parable. Jesus was telling this to God's people, the Jewish people. The Jews were invited to be with God. They initially accepted the offer to be His people, but now, when Jesus comes to say the final preparations are being prepared, they reject the invitation. God's people rejected the son (Jesus). The host went and brought the crippled, the blind, and the lame to his party. He brought the people in who were needy and who were not whole. He said, "I tell you, not one of those men who were invited will get a taste of my banquet." They rejected his invitation and He opened it to those who were ready to accept it. Jesus was telling the Jews, if you religious folks decide not to follow me, the kingdom will be open to the Gentile people. The Gentiles need me and they will be open to coming to me. This passage makes me think: How many of us accept the initial invitation, but are too busy to go to the party? How many of us have said we accept Christ, but our priorities lie elsewhere? We are too busy with the things of the world to follow through with our commitment to Him!

Maybe you accepted the invitation to the party knowing that you have no intention of going. You have no intention of following through with any kind of commitment to Christ. Or maybe, you get caught up in other things that steal your focus from what is truly important. In this parable the host was going to make sure that his house was full. He probably didn't want all of that food and hard work to go to waste. Think about the money that the host must have put into the banquet only to find that the people decided not to attend. Those people didn't take their invitation seriously. Do we take the invitation that God gives us seriously? It didn't cost Him any money to invite us to this great banquet, but it did cost Him the life of His Son Jesus. Religious folks know there is an invitation, but they are just not too concerned about it. Other things are more important. People choose not to come to church because something else seems to be a little more important. I heard someone say once, "You will be surprised who you see and don't see in heaven." Let me tell you people who have had a checkered past come into the church and get on fire for the Lord. They are ready to work and witness; they want to soak up the Word, while those life-long church people are really nonchalant about the things of God. It seems the church people can easily get caught up in other things in their lives.

People Accepted The Invitation

The original guests declined to come to the wedding feast, so now there was all of this food that was going to go to waste. So the king says, "I am not going to waste what I prepared. Invite more people to come." So the servants brought people in off of the streets. Again, Jesus was speaking of the Jews' rejection of God's invitation and the invitation that God ultimately gave to the whole world. You don't have to be a certain gender, a certain race, or be economically well off—everyone who gives his life to Jesus is welcome at the feast of God. These people who are brought in are street people, they are not the wealthy that deserve to eat with the king. The leper, the blind, or the peasant off the street has nothing to offer the king by his presence. This group of guests would not have been invited to a common banquet, let alone to one that is hosted by the king. They are only eating with the king because of His grace towards them.

I have accepted the King's invitation to the party. I'm not invited because I am a preacher. I am completely unworthy of going, but I am going because of His grace towards me. Romans 3:23 says, *"for all have sinned and fall short of the glory of God..."* I have to come to terms with the fact that I am a sinner. I fall short of God's standard. But grace makes up the difference. None of us deserves to sit at His banquet table. We all deserve the fires of hell because of our sin, for our rebellion against God. But through the cross of Jesus, the banquet table is open for a sinner like me!

This reminds me of a song by the group Mercy Me. The song is called, <u>I Can Only Imagine</u>. It is hard to comprehend what God has prepared for us. I have been invited to some impressive feasts before, been to some good buffets, but they all pale in comparison to the Wedding Feast of God because this feast is going to be catered by the King of Kings and Lord of Lords. God made this whole world in six days…just imagine what the party at the end of time is going to be like!

People Didn't Take The Invitation Seriously

As the host came and greeted his guests, he noticed one man who was not wearing the wedding clothes. It was the custom for the king to provide the guests with wedding garments. This would have definitely been needed in this case because the people who are there are poor people off of the streets. This man intrigues me the most in this parable. Everyone took the wedding clothes but him. He accepted the invitation to the party, but rejected the clothes he needed to wear to be there. Could you imagine being invited to be a part of a wedding, and they even bought you a tux to wear to the event? What type of a reaction would you receive if you showed up in your shorts and a Hawaiian shirt? They paid a huge price for you to wear the wedding garment and you decided, "I don't want to wear it." That is the way it is with us in our Christian walks with God. When we accept Jesus into our lives, we say, "I want to be at this great feast at the end of time." At that time we are given clothing that we need to wear. Isaiah 61:10 says, *"I delight greatly in the Lord; my soul rejoices in my God. For he has clothed me with garments of salvation and arrayed me in a robe of righteousness..."* God didn't give us literal clothing. It's not as if you have to wear a Jesus t-shirt or you are not a Christian. No, He gives us garments of salvation, a robe of righteousness to wear. The way we live our lives, the character we possess is the clothing that He wants to give us. In the book of Zechariah 3:3 it says, *"Now Joshua was dressed in filthy clothes as he stood before the angel. The angel said to those who were standing before him, 'take off his filthy clothes.' Then he said to Joshua, 'See, I have taken away your sin, and I will put rich garments on you."* We all, because of our sin, are dressed in filthy rags, but God desires to dress us in garments of salvation (spotless pure robes of white).

Why in the world would I want to continue to be dressed in my filthy robes, when there are nice new robes available? When we make the decision to accept Christ, accept His invitation to the party—we should dress for the party! Live your life dressed in His righteousness.

The Bible says that there are people who think they are going to the party, but are not going to make it in. Matthew

7:21 says, *"Not everyone who says to me, 'Lord, Lord,' will enter the kingdom of heaven, but only he who does the will of my Father who is in heaven."* Are you wearing the appropriate clothes to make it into the party? If not, then take a look at what happens to those who are not dressed properly for the party. Verse 13 of Matthew 22 says, *"Then the king told the attendants, Tie him hand and foot, and throw him outside, into the darkness, where there will be weeping and gnashing of teeth."* This is a warning about hell. It is described here as darkness, weeping and gnashing of teeth—other places in the Bible describe hell as a fire that never goes out, and the worm that never dies. This is not a place that you want to be. You either go to the party and have eternal life, or you are locked out of the party and have eternal torment. Just like the opening story—I'm willing to give by faith what I have now—to possess the abundance that is just beyond my sight.

My question to you as you read this today: Which one of these people are you? Have you rejected God's invitation or have you accepted it? You can know right now, without a doubt, that you are going to this feast. If you believe that Jesus died for your sins, and you desire to live for Him…you are saved. How do I know that? Because 1 John 1:9 says, *"If we confess our sins, he is faithful and just and will forgive us of our sins and purify us from all unrighteousness."* No matter how bad your sins are, Jesus' blood can cover them all. All it takes is a desire from you to want to change your life and to be committed to following Jesus. Accept Him, and then dress your life appropriately for the party!

PART 2

THE SACRIFICIAL KING

Surely He took up our infirmities and carried our sorrows, yet we considered him stricken by God, smitten by him, and afflicted. But he was pierced for our transgressions, he was crushed for our iniquities; the punishment that brought us peace was upon him, and by his wounds we are healed. We all, like sheep, have gone astray, each of us has turned to his own way; and the LORD has laid on him the iniquity of us all. He was oppressed and afflicted, yet he did not open his mouth; he was led like a lamb to the slaughter, and as a sheep before her shearers is silent, so he did not open his mouth.

Isaiah 53: 4-7

Humble King To Conquering King

THE LORD'S SUPPER

My cousin's daughter Kathy usually stays in children's church on Sunday mornings, but one Sunday she went with her parents to the regular adult service. When Communion was served, she turned to her mother and whispered loudly, 'The snack in children's church is much better. And we get a lot more juice.'"[17]

Obviously there is so much more to the Lord's Supper than that. The Lord's Supper is a very serious and holy time for followers of Jesus. In Luke 22, we read about the meaning of this sacred event.

> [7] Then came the day of Unleavened Bread on which the Passover lamb had to be sacrificed. [8] Jesus sent Peter and John, saying, "Go and make preparations for us to eat the Passover."
>
> [9] "Where do you want us to prepare for it?" they asked.
>
> [10] He replied, "As you enter the city, a man carrying a jar of water will meet you. Follow him to the house that he enters, [11] and say to the owner of the house, 'The Teacher asks: Where is the guest room, where I may eat the

Passover with my disciples?' [12] *He will show you a large upper room, all furnished. Make preparations there."*

[13] *They left and found things just as Jesus had told them. So they prepared the Passover.*

[14] *When the hour came, Jesus and his apostles reclined at the table.* [15] *And he said to them, "I have eagerly desired to eat this Passover with you before I suffer.* [16] *For I tell you, I will not eat it again until it finds fulfillment in the kingdom of God."*

[17] *After taking the cup, he gave thanks and said, "Take this and divide it among you.* [18] *For I tell you I will not drink again of the fruit of the vine until the kingdom of God comes."*

[19] *And he took bread, gave thanks and broke it, and gave it to them, saying, "This is my body given for you; do this in remembrance of me."*

[20] *In the same way, after the supper he took the cup, saying, "This cup is the new covenant in my blood, which is poured out for you.* [21] *But the hand of him who is going to betray me is with mine on the table.* [22] *The Son of Man will go as it has been decreed, but woe to that man who betrays him."* [23] *They began to question among themselves which of them it might be who would do this.*

In this passage, Jesus and His disciples gather together for the Passover meal. There are a lot of interesting things about the Passover, but there are three things that I want to point out in this chapter.

Remember What God Has Done

The Passover was a feast that the Israelites were to celebrate as a reminder of what God had done for them. In the Old Testament, God's people (Israel) were in slavery in Egypt. God called Moses from the desert to go and bring His people out of Egypt. So Moses went, but Egypt's leader would not let Israel go because they were useful to him as slaves. So God sent great plagues on the land. God turned all the water to blood in Egypt. He sent plagues of frogs, gnats, flies, and locusts. He sent hail and a plague on their livestock and struck the people with boils. He also sent darkness on Egypt. None of those caused Egypt to let God's people go. So God had one final plague that He was going to send to the Egyptians. He was going to kill the firstborn in every family in Egypt.

God told the Israelites to kill a lamb and spread its blood around the doorframes of their houses. They were told that when the destroying angel came, the angel would see the blood and pass over their houses. So all of the houses that had the blood of the lamb on the doorframes of their houses, were passed over by the angel. The firstborn in these homes were not killed. However, the firstborn were killed in all of the houses that didn't have blood on the door frames. After the Egyptians saw what happened, they let Israel leave. God got them out of slavery because of this event. This is why the event was called the Passover; because the angel passed over them and delivered them out of slavery. After God brought them out of Egypt, He told them, "Each year you are to hold a festival and come together as a people and remember how I rescued you from slavery in Egypt." In Exodus 13:10, God says, *"You must keep this ordinance at the appointed time year after year."* So that is what Jesus is celebrating with His disciples in this passage. He is remembering the great things God has done for them in the past.

But during this Passover with His disciples, Jesus introduces a different kind of remembrance. "You are no longer to focus upon how God brought you out of slavery in Egypt, but now you are to focus upon how my death is going to bring you out of your slavery to sin." Jesus takes the bread and breaks it and gives it to His followers…and says, *"This is my body given for you; do this in remembrance of me."* Then He takes the cup and says, *"This cup is the new covenant in my blood, which is poured out for you."* Jesus is pointing to the cross, where His body is broken and His blood is spilled for us. Jesus is the new Passover lamb. <u>His blood saves us.</u>

In the Old Testament God had strict laws on which lambs could be used for the Passover. In Exodus 12:46 God says, *"It must be eaten inside one house; take none of the meat outside the house. Do not break any of the bones."* The last line says, "Do not break any bones on the Passover lamb."

When Jesus was on the cross, the soldiers came around and broke the legs of the thief on each side of Jesus so that they would die more quickly. But when they came to Jesus, He was already dead, so they did not break His legs. No bone was broken in our Passover lamb, just as the law required.

The law also required the lamb to be perfect. Exodus 12:5 says, *"The animals you choose must be year—old males without defect, and you may take them from the sheep or the goats."* Jesus also fulfilled that verse as our Passover lamb. He was perfect. He had no flaws—He had no sin. Peter, who sat at the table with Jesus that night, identifies Jesus as our new Passover lamb. In 1 Peter 1:18-19 he says, *"For you know that it was not with perishable things such as silver or gold that you were redeemed from the empty way of life handed down to you from your forefathers, but with the precious blood of Christ, a lamb without blemish or defect."* Jesus was the new Passover lamb that died to save us from our sins. In the Old Testament people had to sacrifice lambs year after year for the sins that they committed. But Jesus died once and for all. We don't have to sacrifice animals each year for our forgiveness; Jesus took care of that. Jesus told the disciples, and He tells us today, to remember this sacrifice. Remember what God has done for you to free you from your sins.

The people of Israel came together as a people to celebrate the Exodus; celebrating the Passover was a community event. So we too come together as a people to celebrate the cross as one people. Can you just imagine growing up in an Israelite home? The kids are going to wonder why in the world do we slaughter a lamb and why is there a festival every year. God tells the Israelites in Exodus 13:14, *"In days to come, when your son asks you, 'what does this mean?' say to him, 'With a mighty hand the Lord brought us out of Egypt, out of the land of slavery.'"* Obviously, their kids are going to be curious about why they are doing this. This is an opportunity for them to teach their children what God did for them in bringing them out of slavery in Egypt. In the same way, we partake in communion as a remembrance of the cross and what Jesus has done for us, and our kids may ask us, "Mom, Dad, why do you drink grape juice and eat bread?" This is a great opportunity to teach our kids about what Jesus has done for us, how He died on the cross to save us from our sins. Continue to remember what Jesus has done for you. Continue to come together to celebrate the deliverance we have from sin.

God Was Obviously In Control

There was no doubt God was in control back in Egypt. God performed ten miraculous plagues to bring out His people. Everything worked out perfectly according to His plan. And, in today's passage, we see that Jesus is totally in control of this Passover. During the Passover feast, Jerusalem would double in size. It would be wall to wall people because everyone wanted to come to the Holy City and celebrate this great festival. So Jerusalem was packed and so were all the towns that were close to Jerusalem. Jesus says to the disciples, "Oh, by the way, go find us a place to celebrate the Passover feast tonight." I can imagine the disciples were thinking, "Yeah, right. Like we are going to be able to find anything this late." That is like getting Cubs World Series tickets the day of the game. It just isn't going to happen. The odds of finding a place anywhere close to Jerusalem the day of the feast are impossible. All of the hotels and banquet halls had to be filled. But Jesus gives them detailed instructions in Luke 22:10-11. *"As you enter the city, a man carrying a jar of water will meet you. Follow him to the house that he enters, and say to the owner of the house, 'The Teacher asks: Where is the guest room, where I may eat the Passover with my disciples?'"* Again the disciples are probably shaking their heads. Like there is going to be a man carrying a jar of water. Carrying water was a woman's job in this culture. But they went and wouldn't you know it, it happened just as Jesus said that it would. They saw a man and followed him and he had a room for them to celebrate the feast. Jesus was in control. He knew how everything was going to fall into place. God knew from the beginning of time how it was all going to play out. 1 Peter 1:20 says, *"He (Jesus) was chosen before the creation of the world, but was revealed in these last times for your sake."* Before He created the world, God knew He was going to have to send His son into the world to be the Passover sacrifice for us. God is not up in heaven panicking, saying, "Oh no, what now? I guess the only thing left to do is to send my son." God is completely in control.

The Passover Has Judgment In It

The Egyptians where judged and killed because they did not have the blood over their doors. The people with blood over their doors were considered innocent. The destroying angel didn't stop at every house and weigh the option, "Should I destroy the firstborn of this household or not? How good or bad has this family been?" No, the only consideration was whether or not the house had blood on it. If it had blood, then the residents escaped the judgment of God. If the Egyptians would have caught word of what the Israelites were doing, feared the Lord enough and put blood over their doors—they would have been saved. The opposite is also true. If the Israelites would have thought to themselves, "This is a bunch of baloney. How can blood of a lamb spread over my door save me? I am not going to do this foolishness." Even though they were God's people, judgment would have fallen on them. The angel didn't go to the Israelite subdivision and say, well every other house has blood on it except these two, but this is the Israelite part of town, I will spare them. No, the only factor that mattered to the destroying angel was the blood.

It is the same today as well. There will be a day when we will stand before God. 2 Corinthians 5:10 says, *"For we must all appear before the judgment seat of Christ, that each one may receive what is due him for the things done while in the body, whether good or bad."* If our lives are covered with the blood of Christ, we will live. If we don't have the blood of Christ over our lives, we will face eternal punishment. What matters is the blood! It doesn't matter how rich you are or how smart you are. It doesn't matter how many good works you have done in your life or how many times you have been to church. We have all sinned, we are all flawed, and the only thing that can save us is the blood of Christ. If you decide you are not going to trust in Jesus' blood and say, "How can His blood save me?", that is your choice. But Jesus came to save us from the wrath of God.

Luke 22:20 says, *"In the same way, after the supper he took the cup, saying, 'This cup is the new covenant in my blood, which is poured out for you.'"* Jesus tells us that His blood is the cup of a new covenant. "Covenant" means agreement between two parties. Through the blood of Jesus, God made a <u>new</u> <u>covenant</u> with man. It is no longer based on the law which man cannot keep, but it is based on the work of the cross. And if we enter into the covenant walk with God through the cross, we have no need to fear. One of my favorite verses is Romans 8:1. *"Therefore, there is now no condemnation for those who are in Christ Jesus..."* There is no condemnation; there is no judgment, if you are in the new covenant that God made with man through the cross. The only thing that matters is the blood!

Remain In Me

As I am writing this book, I am looking at a power strip on my desk. I have my lamp, printer, computer, phone and electric pencil sharpener all plugged into this power strip. If I would go to the wall outlet, and unplug the power strip, would my lamp work? Or my printer? No, there would be no electricity running to anything that is plugged into the power strip. Picture your life as a power strip. By ourselves we can do nothing, but if we are plugged into Jesus, our power source, we can get the power to do the things that we need to do in our lives. John 15 says,

> [1] *"I am the true vine, and my Father is the gardener.* [2] *He cuts off every branch in me that bears no fruit, while every branch that does bear fruit he prunes so that it will be even more fruitful.* [3] *You are already clean because of the word I have spoken to you.* [4] *Remain in me, and I will remain in you. No branch can bear fruit by itself; it must remain in the vine. Neither can you bear fruit unless you remain in me.*
>
> [5] *"I am the vine; you are the branches. If*

a man remains in me and I in him, he will bear much fruit; apart from me you can do nothing. ⁶ If anyone does not remain in me, he is like a branch that is thrown away and withers; such branches are picked up, thrown into the fire and burned. ⁷ If you remain in me and my words remain in you, ask whatever you wish, and it will be given you. ⁸ This is to my Father's glory, that you bear much fruit, showing yourselves to be my disciples.

Separation Brings Death

This passage really comes to light when you look at it in the context that it is in. This is the last night that Jesus was spending with His disciples before His death. Jesus just enjoyed the Passover feast with His disciples, He washed their feet, and He led them in the Lord's supper. The last sentence in John chapter 14 says, *"Come, now; let us leave."* They were leaving the upper room and they were heading for the Garden of Gethsemane where Jesus will be arrested, and He will be led to the cross to die. As they walked from the upper room toward the Garden of Gethsemane, they would no doubt be among vineyards. It was the time of year when grape vines would be beginning to blossom. The object lesson was right in front of the disciples to see. Jesus was very good at putting a mental picture in the minds of the people as He taught. This teaching of Jesus in John 15 has a theme that jumps out of the page at you. "Remain in me." He says it four times in these eight verses. He uses the word "remain" six times. And if you read on in this passage, He says it several more times.

Why was Jesus stressing "remain in me" so much? Because this was a message that the disciples really needed to hear! <u>Within a couple of hours</u>, Jesus would be taken from them and they would have to choose whether they would continue to follow Him or turn away. This night, this weekend, was a critical point for the disciples. Judas chose not to remain in Jesus. He cared more for the wealth of the world and turned Jesus in for 30 pieces of silver. The disciples were all faced with a choice when Jesus was being arrested, and they all ran and left Jesus by Himself. Peter had a choice to remain in Jesus, yet he confessed three times, "I don't know this Jesus you are talking about." It didn't look like the disciples did too good of a job remaining in Him. What about us? We desperately need to hear this teaching as well. Every day, we have so many choices to reject Jesus and follow the pattern of the world. Choose Jesus or choose all of these material possessions. Choose Jesus or choose this bad relationship. It is decision time; will we remain in Him?

The disciples didn't know they were going to face a huge trial later that night. It surprised them. Neither do we know when we are going to face some difficult situations in our lives. We need to remain in Him, so that when trials come we are ready to face them. Otherwise when trials come, we may run from God. The disciples had a bad couple of days— Jesus' arrest, death, burial. However, they were willing to turn back to Jesus and die for Him. They were willing to do that because of their strong relationship with Him. Maybe a few people reading this book have strayed a bit. Things have come up in your life where you have been hiding out doing other things. Now is the time to turn back and live for the Lord. It is not too late to recommit your life to Him.

In verse 5 Jesus says, *"I am the vine, you are the branches. If a man remains in me and I in him, he will bear much fruit; apart from me you can do nothing."* Jesus is the vine, we are the branches. We all know that a branch has to remain in the vine to keep living. You separate a branch from the vine, it dies. It gets its nutrients, its very life from the vine. So Jesus tells us that our life is dependent on staying connected to Him. In the chapter before this passage, John 14:6, Jesus says, *"I am the way and the truth and the life. No one comes to the Father except through me."* Our sin separates us from God, so the only way we can remain in Him is to receive the work He did for us on the cross. We need to remain in Him if we want to go to heaven and have eternal life. You must be in the vine to have life.

An interesting point about the vine and the branches is that a branch will never become independent from the vine. When a child is conceived, it is totally dependent on the nourishment of its mother in the womb for 9 months. For some time after that, it is dependent on the mom for food to eat. But once the child is weaned, it eventually starts to become more and more independent, until eventually it does not need the mother anymore. Not so with this illustration with the branches. A branch will be as completely dependent on the nutrients coming from the vine when the branch is 50 years old as it is when it is one day old. The branches always need the vine, just like we always need Jesus.

Jesus makes it very clear that life is in Him, and in Him alone. You can't substitute anything else for the vine. There is no substitute for being connected to Jesus. If you are not connected to Jesus, look at what happens: John 15:6, *"If anyone does not remain in me, he is like a branch that is thrown away and withers; such branches are picked up, thrown into the fire and burned."* This is not a pretty picture. It is a picture of hell. If we do not remain in Him, we die and will be thrown into hell. This is a very big warning for us that we need to be bearing fruit and not just playing religion. There were several times when Jesus accused the Pharisees, the religious leaders, of not bearing fruit. These people were at the temple all the time; they read their Bibles, they gave the required money…but they didn't have a change of attitude and did not have a love for God or a love for their neighbors. It was all about them and the things that they did.

Let me give you an example that kind of puts you in God's shoes. Let's say that you planted a bunch of tomato plants and you are anxious to eat some good tomatoes. But you go out to the garden and all that you find is a bunch of beautiful green tomato plants. No tomatoes. Will you be satisfied with just having pretty green tomato plants? I doubt it. You didn't plant the tomato plants to get the plant, but the fruit. In our Christian walk, have we become content in just having a plant? Are we concerned with bearing fruit? Are we content coming to church, maybe listening to Christian radio, but making no behavioral changes in our lives? If you are not bearing fruit you are not doing what you should be doing.

Luke 13:6-8 says, *"Then he (Jesus) told this parable: A man had a fig tree, planted in his vineyard, and he went to look for fruit on it, but did not find any. So he said to the man who took care of the vineyard, For three years now I've been coming to look for fruit on this fig tree and haven't found any. Cut it down! Why should it use up the soil? Sir, the man replied, leave it alone for one more year, and I'll dig around it and fertilize it. If it bears fruit next year, fine! If not, then cut it down."* God doesn't want a Christian in name only, He wants someone who will remain in Him and bear fruit. When God comes to look for fruit in your life, will He find any? Tomato plants are useless if they don't have tomatoes on them. Christians are useless if they are not bearing Christ-like fruit in their lives.

Remaining In Him Brings A Life Change

Read verse 5 of John 15 again. Jesus says, *"I am the vine, you are the branches. If a man remains in me and I in him, he will bear much fruit; apart from me you can do nothing."* Is it possible for Him to remain in us, at the same time we remain in Him?

Several years ago a blacksmith gave his testimony to a man who was in his shop. He ended by saying, "I'm glad I'm in Christ and that Christ is in me." The next day this man came by the blacksmith shop and said, "I have been thinking. I don't think it's possible for you to be in Christ and Christ to be in you." At that time the blacksmith had a horseshoe in the fire so he asked the man if the horseshoe was in the fire. The man replied, "Yes, it is." Then the blacksmith took the shoe out of the fire and held it close to the man and asked, "Is the horseshoe in the fire, or is the fire in the horseshoe?"[18]

The blacksmith made his point. That horseshoe was affected by the fire because it sat in the fire for some time. Do you think that the horseshoe would have fire in it if the blacksmith put it in the fire for only two seconds and pulled it out? No. The fire was put into the horseshoe because the horseshoe sat in the fire for some time. Are you seeing the parallel here? Christ is in us not because we come to church for an hour each Sunday, but Christ is in us because we spend a lot of time in Him. When we spend time with Christ, it affects us. In the Old Testament, there is a story of Moses going up the mountain to see the Lord. Exodus 34:29 says, *"When Moses came down from Mount Sinai with the two tablets of the Testimony in his hands, he was not aware that his face was radiant because he had spoken with the Lord."* Because Moses spent time in the presence of God the appearance of his face changed. This happened many times. Each time Moses spoke with the Lord, his face would be radiant. The people knew without a doubt Moses had been with God. When we spend time with God, it changes us also. People can tell we are different. We are not lifeless, fruitless branches like those we read about in John 15. We bear much fruit for God. We display the fruit of the Spirit in our lives. We have love, joy, peace, patience, kindness, goodness, faithfulness, gentleness and self-control. Our lives are radiant in this dark world.

Go back to the story of the horseshoe; when the horseshoe has the fire in it, it can be formed. The blacksmith can hammer out any problem spots. When we have Christ in us, we can be formed. Jesus can take our hearts and cut out any sin. In this passage it says we are pruned. Verse 2 of John 15 says, *"He cuts off every branch in me that bears no fruit, while every branch that does bear fruit he prunes so that it will be even more fruitful."* We carry over into our Christian lives a lot of things from our old lives that are not Christ-like. We bring a lot of sinful luggage into our relationship with Jesus but He accepts us in His grace. He does not expect us to "clean up our act" before coming to Him. He welcomes us even though we have those sinful traits, or "dead branches" in our lives. But through the process of sanctification, God cuts the "old self" out of our lives. He cleans us up. He prunes us. It doesn't happen suddenly, or once and for all, but it takes a whole lifetime. He does it repeatedly and often. Slowly and surely God's Word is at work in our hearts, cleansing us from the bad so that we can bear fruit in our lives. A gardener continually prunes the same plant year after year after year. God continually prunes and cleanses our lives from the things that will not bear fruit for His kingdom.

God wants to come in and take out the bad habits and replace them with good habits, habits from His Word. He wants to prune us to set us free so that we can become more healthy and more fruitful. He doesn't prune us to hurt us, but to help us. We hold on tightly to some things in our lives because we think we are wise. We won't say it, but sometimes we think we are wiser than God's Word. "I know my situation…if I hold on to more of my money, I will have more." But the opposite is true. Tithing gives you more. Think of tithing like pruning. Let me describe a little bit about pruning. You have to cut the bad to make room for more of the good and to get more nutrients to the good part of the tree. Sounds logical. But then comes what may seem to be the illogical part: you also need to get rid of some of the good buds on the tree to make the other good buds better. If you do not prune you may have 100 apples on a tree, but they will be very small apples. They have to share the nutrients. If you prune the tree and get rid of half of the good buds, it may seem like a waste, but in the long run you will bear better fruit. Instead of getting 100 apples, you will only get 50 apples, but these 50 apples will be much bigger because they will get more nutrients. When you consider weight, you will be better off having 50 big apples than 100 small apples. There will be more fruit in the 50 apples.

Some of us try to hold on to things because it makes sense to us, but we are far better off to let go and give these things to God. One hundred apples sound far better to most of us than 50 apples. That is because we don't understand pruning. Once we understand the benefits of pruning, we will be willing to do it. Be willing to sacrifice and go for the big fruit. Don't stay as you are in your life and be content with the small fruit. God wants to bring freedom to different areas of your life. In using the example of tithing, we hold on to our money; unwilling to give it away. We must see that this will result in bearing small fruit. We need to be willing to prune what we have, then what we do have will be even more fruitful. God will *"open the floodgates of heaven and pour out so much blessing that you will not have room enough for it."*[19]

We must learn that we have to remain in Christ and follow His Word if we want to bear fruit. When a true believer is made aware of any area of his life that is not yielded to Christ, he will yield it. If He is not in your life, you will not bear fruit. As John 15:5 says, *"You can do nothing."* Let's pretend I have a plastic glove. What can the plastic glove do on its own? Let me give it some commands. "Pick up the Bible." "Draw a circle." "Wave to the crowd." It can't do anything that I told it to do. Now imagine what happens when I put my hand in it. The glove can now pick up the Bible. It can draw a circle. It can wave. When my hand is in the glove it can do all sorts of things. When my hand is not in the glove, it is helpless. When God's hand is in our lives, watch out—anything is possible. But if we don't remain in Him, we are like lifeless gloves.

When the glove is waving and picking up the Bible and drawing a circle…who gets the credit for that, the glove or my hand? Of course the hand is the one that gets the credit. When we do things for the Lord, do we get the credit, or does the credit go to God? In verse 8 Jesus says, *"This is to my Father's glory, that you bear much fruit, showing yourselves to be my disciples."* The glory goes to God when we bear fruit and do things for His kingdom. If people hear a good sermon, the pastor doesn't get the glory—God gets the glory because the people take that Word and live it out in their lives.

Some people may think bearing fruit is hard, only super Christians can do that. But fruit bearing is for all Christians. Fruit bearing is not that difficult. It requires only one thing. What is that one thing? To remain in Jesus. If a branch remains in the vine, it will automatically bear fruit. It is a natural thing. The only requirement for a branch is to remain connected to the vine. When we stay connected to our vine and read His Word, and when we are people of prayer… the fruit of God will undoubtedly be displayed in our lives.

I hope that you want your life to be loaded with fruit, because that brings Him glory. 1 Corinthians 10:31 says, *"So whether you eat or drink or whatever you do, do it all for the glory of God."* Everything you do, do it to bring glory to God. Every genuine branch wants to honor the Lord. <u>People who are saved by Grace cares more about the glory of God than they do about themselves</u>. If bringing glory to God is your heart's desire, you will learn the secret of remaining in the vine.

Prayers Of Jesus

There is a cartoon with a pastor on the phone: "Bad news, Bishop. Our church planting team is divided on whether to call the new congregation 'First United Church' or 'United First Church.'"[20] We can laugh at a little cartoon like that, but the point it gets across is not so funny. As Jesus' followers, sometimes we disagree on the silliest things. The night before Jesus died, He was in the garden praying. In John 17, we see that He prays for the future church. This is only a portion of Jesus' prayer that night, but it shows His longing for the church.

> [20] "My prayer is not for them alone. I pray also for those who will believe in me through their message, [21] that all of them may be one, Father, just as you are in me and I am in you. May they also be in us so that the world may believe that you have sent me. [22] I have given them the glory that you gave me, that they may be one as we are one: [23] I in them and you in me. May they be brought to complete unity to let the world know that you sent me and have loved them even as you have loved me.

[24] *"Father, I want those you have given me to be with me where I am, and to see my glory, the glory you have given me because you loved me before the creation of the world.*

[25] *"Righteous Father, though the world does not know you, I know you, and they know that you have sent me.* [26] *I have made you known to them, and will continue to make you known in order that the love you have for me may be in them and that I myself may be in them."*

Jesus Prayer For Future Believers

Jesus prays with one overall theme, "unity between believers." Verse 21 says, *"that all of them may be one."* What did He mean by us being one? One Sunday morning a minister gave a sermon to all of the young children. A bright-eyed three-year-old girl listened intently as he explained that God wanted them all to get along and love each other. "God wants us all to be one," he said. To which the little girl replied, "But I don't want to be one. I want to be four!"[21] She didn't quite get the meaning behind, "us all being one."

We understand unity. We at least know what we ought to do. The problem is when the unity comes at a high cost to ourselves. We have to sacrifice our opinions and desires to keep unity. Sometimes you will have to give in and let the building committee pick out the carpet instead of the tile you want for the church foyer. You will have to go with the flow on which song the praise team wants to sing, even though you wanted to sing different songs. You will occasionally have to lay aside your opinions for the good of God's kingdom. But we should never sacrifice Biblical truth to keep unity! You need to stick to scriptures even if it will ruffle a few feathers. I don't care who gets offended and leaves the church when we hold to the truth, "Jesus is the only way to heaven." "Sex is only between one man and one woman who are in the covenant relationship of marriage." Unity is not found in accepting everything! Unity is found in living out the truth that we find in Jesus!

A watching world will see how we respond to each other in the Body of Christ. How tragic it is when Christians fight over irrelevant things like the color of the carpet in the sanctuary, or how many cupboards should be put in the church kitchen. Sometimes we fight over the silliest stuff that has no eternal value whatsoever. Unity is very important to Jesus. How important is unity? In this short prayer of seven verses that Jesus has for the future church, He mentions the theme of unity three times. Verse 21, *"that all of them may be one."* Verse 22, *"that they may be one."* Verse 23, *"May they be brought to complete unity."* Not brought to unity, but to complete unity. Perfect unity. Do you see what He compares our unity to? He compares it to the unity He has with the Father. He says, *"That they* (meaning all of us) *may be one as we* (Jesus & the Father) *are one."* Jesus is setting His expectations of us at a high level.

How can we be one? There is only one way. Verse 22, *"I have given them the glory that you gave me, that they may be one as we are one."* We can be one through the glory

Jesus has given us. It is only by the indwelling of His Spirit. It is God's spirit inside of us…His Spirit of love, peace and forgiveness that saturates our being. If God's Spirit is in you and God's Spirit is in me, we can be one. But if one of us is not living our life controlled by the Spirit, there is a good chance that the unity will be broken. God's Spirit living inside of us is the only possible way for us to be one. If we let our own thoughts, or our own opinions control us—we will never be one—because there is always going to be someone who disagrees with our opinions. The key to unity is the common spirit of Christ inside of us. If I have Christ in me it changes the way I view things, it changes the way I handle things, it changes how I feel about other people.

The point Jesus is making here is that the oneness we experience with Him <u>should lead</u> to a oneness we can experience with each other. John makes this point many times in the book of 1 John. One of those verses is 1 John 4:20, *"if anyone says, I love God, yet hates his brother, he is a liar. For anyone who does not love his brother, whom he has seen, cannot love God, whom he has not seen."* If we don't love our brother we cannot love God. There is a correlation between how we treat each other and how we treat God.

A young lady named Sally took a seminary class taught by Professor Smith, who was known for his elaborate object lessons. One day Sally walked into class to find a large target placed on the wall, with several darts resting on a nearby table. Professor Smith told the students to draw a picture of someone they disliked or someone who had made them very angry—and he would allow them to throw darts at the person's picture. Sally's friend (on her right), drew a picture of another woman who had stolen her boyfriend. Another friend (on her left), drew a picture of his younger brother. Sally drew a picture of Professor Smith. The class lined up and began throwing darts with much laughter, enjoying the thought of bringing pain to the person they had hard feelings for. Some of the students threw with such force that they ripped apart their targets. Sally, looking forward to her turn, was filled with disappointment when Professor Smith asked the students to return to their seats so he could begin his lecture. As Sally fumed about missing her chance to throw the darts, the professor began removing the target from the wall. Underneath the target was a picture of Jesus. A hush fell over the room as each student viewed the mangled image of their Savior—holes and jagged marks covered his face. His eyes were virtually pierced out. The professor said only these words, *"Inasmuch as ye have done it unto the least of these my brethren, ye have done it unto me."*[22]

When we do something to someone else…just picture that you are doing it to Jesus. Whether it is good or bad. That should get us to act differently. Instead of yelling at your brother, you are yelling at Jesus. Instead of cheating your brother, you are cheating Jesus. When we are so slow to love other people, we are slow to love God. We say, "I love God," yet we hold grudges against other people. As a church we build walls between each other instead of tearing them down.

Why is it so important for us to be united and show love for one another? In verse 23 Jesus says, *"May they be brought to complete unity to let the world know that you sent me."* Unity is important so people can see that Jesus is God and was sent from God. When we go around arguing and being bitter towards each other and talking bad about each other…people outside the church are not very impressed with the God we serve. We are called by His name, "Christians". If we don't watch our actions, we will be a poor reflection of Him, and people will not want to know Him. How we treat one another will bring people to Christ or push them away. If you wanted to join an organization, would you join one where people argued all of the time, or would you join an organization where the people stand together and value each other.

Let me tell you, when Christians are one with Christ and one with each other, the growth of the church is inevitable. Just like in the book of Acts…they grew in number daily. They had a strong relationship with Christ and they wanted everybody, no matter how different from themselves, to be a part of their group. How about us? Do differences scare us?

Do we try to keep the people who are different from us at an arm's length?

There was a college student named Bill who recently became a believer while attending a campus Bible study. Bill had wild hair, and his wardrobe was jeans and a T-shirt with holes in it. Across from campus is a well-dressed, very conservative church. One Sunday Bill decides to go there. He walks in late and shoeless. The sanctuary is packed. Bill heads down the aisle looking for a seat. Having nearly reached the pulpit, he realizes there are no empty seats, so he squats down on the carpet. The congregation is feeling very uncomfortable. This guy is so much different than them. About that time…from the back of the church, a gray-haired elder in a three-piece suit starts walking toward Bill with a cane. With all eyes focused on the developing drama, the minister waits to begin his sermon until the elder does what he has to do. The elderly man gets to where Bill was sitting on the floor, he drops his cane on the floor and with great difficulty lowers himself to sit next to Bill. The minister begins to speak, "What I'm about to preach, you'll never remember. What you've just seen, you'll never forget."[23]

People remember acts of acceptance, acts of unity. People will remember you hugging and loving the unlovable. How do we respond to differences in the church, whether they be a difference of appearance or opinion? Do we isolate people different than us—make them feel uncomfortable because they are not like us? Jesus accepted us. We need to reach out and accept others.

Jesus' Prayer For Deliverance

We see another prayer of Jesus in Luke 22:42-44. This is not a prayer for the church, this is a prayer for Himself. Jesus said, *"'Father, if you are willing, take this cup from me; yet not my will, but yours be done.' An angel from heaven appeared to him and strengthened him. And being in anguish, he prayed more earnestly, and his sweat was like drops of blood falling to the ground."* We see in this passage, Jesus was not looking forward to the cross. Jesus was fully human and fully God. The fully human part of Jesus did not want to suffer the extreme pain that He was going to face the next day on the cross. He was totally aware of the painful sacrifice that was coming His way the next day.

Jesus prays, *"Father, take this cup from me."* The cup that Jesus is talking about is the suffering that He was going to have to face. Jesus did not want to die. This was not His definition of fun or something that He looked forward to. In Matthew 26 we see that Jesus prays three times to the Father to see if there is a way out. He was in so much anguish that He was sweating drops of blood. Nothing in His physical self wanted to go to the cross.

But Jesus being fully God, as well as fully human, knew what needed to be done. Each time He prayed for the cup to pass, He always ended His prayers by saying, *"Your will be done."* He knew it was the Father's will, and He knew this was the very reason He came into the world. He came into the world to die upon the cross and save us from our sins.

I hear so often in people's lives, "I don't feel like doing this." It could be that they don't feel like going to church, or don't feel like reading their Bible, or don't feel like serving in the church. Just remember, if Jesus did only what He felt like doing, we would still be dead in our sins. He didn't feel like going to the cross, yet He went anyway. In response to His act of love to us, shouldn't we also do things that we don't want to do for Him? The sacrifice He is calling you to make cannot be near as large as the sacrifice He made on your behalf.

Jesus' Arrest

Sometimes it is easy for us to proclaim Jesus as king. Things in life are good, and we know Jesus is on His throne and in control. But there may be other times when we question, "Is God really in control while all of these bad things are happening to me; while all of these bad things are happening in the world." The disciples probably had the same questions. I'm sure that they had no doubt that Jesus was king and that He was in control when He came riding into Jerusalem on a donkey a few days earlier. They saw people coming to Jesus praising Him as their king. But a few days later, the disciples might have been wondering, "Is Jesus really in control?" John 18 gives us insight on whether Jesus is in control even in the bad times.

> *[1] When he had finished praying, Jesus left with his disciples and crossed the Kidron Valley. On the other side there was an olive grove, and he and his disciples went into it.*
>
> *[2] Now Judas, who betrayed him, knew the place, because Jesus had often met there with his disciples. [3] So Judas came to the grove, guiding a detachment of soldiers and some*

officials from the chief priests and Pharisees. They were carrying torches, lanterns and weapons.

⁴ *Jesus, knowing all that was going to happen to him, went out and asked them, "Who is it you want?"*

⁵ *"Jesus of Nazareth," they replied.*

"I am he," Jesus said. (And Judas the traitor was standing there with them.) ⁶ *When Jesus said, "I am he," they drew back and fell to the ground.*

⁷ *Again he asked them, "Who is it you want?" And they said, "Jesus of Nazareth."*

⁸ *"I told you that I am he," Jesus answered. "If you are looking for me, then let these men go."* ⁹ *This happened so that the words he had spoken would be fulfilled: "I have not lost one of those you gave me."*

¹⁰ *Then Simon Peter, who had a sword, drew it and struck the high priest's servant, cutting off his right ear. (The servant's name was Malchus.)*

¹¹ *Jesus commanded Peter, "Put your sword away! Shall I not drink the cup the Father has given me?"*

Jesus just finished celebrating the Passover Feast with His disciples. At the meal He tried to let His disciples in on what was going to happen. He broke the bread and passed the wine—and said "this is my body…and this is my blood which is shed for you." Jesus was telling them that He was going to die to save them from their sins. I don't think the disciples could comprehend the message Jesus gave them. After the meal Jesus led His disciples out to the garden where a huge group of people would ultimately come to arrest Him. Judas, one of the twelve disciples, led this large detachment of soldiers. It was not 20 or 30 soldiers; from the Greek words in this text scholars believe it was more like several hundred Roman soldiers, accompanied by temple guards and some religious rulers. A lot of people came to make sure Jesus didn't get away. The Jews thought Jesus was a threat and they wanted to take Him out of the picture. So they came to arrest Him.

The overall question here is: Who was in control? At first glance you may say that the large crowd was in control. There were so many of them and they had weapons—what could Jesus and His disciples have done? The crowd had to be in control because at the end of this passage they had Jesus bound up and they were leading Him away for trial. But when we take a closer look, we see that Jesus was really the One in control of this situation.

The Soldiers Bow Before Jesus

Here came this massive crowd to arrest Jesus, confident in their power over Him. Jesus asked the crowd, who do you want? Verse 5 & 6 says, *"Jesus of Nazareth, they replied. I am he, Jesus said. (And Judas the traitor was standing there with them). When Jesus said, I am he, they drew back and fell to the ground."* Jesus said *"I am he."* Something about that small statement made the soldiers fall to their knees. Scholars believe it is because Jesus said, "I am". If you remember back in the Old Testament when God told Moses to go to Egypt and lead the Israelites out of Egypt—Moses asked God, who should I say is sending me? The Lord said, "Tell them I am sent you. I am who I am." God's name is I am. Jesus says many times in the book of John "I am ...something. (bread of life, light of the world, gate, good shepherd)" He is claiming to be God. Now He says this simple phrase "I am he" and soldiers fall to the ground before Him. The people came to arrest a traveling preacher, but they couldn't stand before the words of the King of Kings. Bowing before Jesus was not part of the soldiers plan. It happened involuntarily. The weapons and strength they had in numbers were nothing compared to the word of the All Powerful God.

There is a lesson in here for us all. Philippians 2:7-9 says, *"God has exalted him to the highest place and gave him the name above every name, that at the name of Jesus, every knee should bow in heaven and on earth, and under the earth, and every tongue confess that Jesus Christ is Lord."* Make no mistake about it. There will be a day when every knee will bow before Jesus, whether we do it now voluntarily, or we wait and we do it involuntarily. There are many people in our world today like the soldiers in this passage—they don't plan on bowing before Him, but they will. No matter how strong you are—you don't have a choice. Our strength, our wisdom, the job title that we hold, none of these will help us stand before Jesus on judgment day. Don't trust in who you are, or the power you think you have.

> A captain of a ship looked into the darkness and saw faint lights in the distance. Immediately he got on the radio and said, "Alter your course 10 degree's south, we are coming right at you." A message came back, "Alter your course 10 degrees north." The captain, angered because his command was ignored, sent a second message, "Alter your course 10 degrees south—I am the captain!" Soon he received another message, "Alter your course 10 degrees north—I am seaman third class Jones." Immediately the captain sent a third message, "Alter your course 10 degrees south—I am a battle ship!" Then came the reply, "Alter your course 10 degrees north—I am a lighthouse."[24]

The captain thought he was a big man on a big battleship, and that everyone else had to alter their course and make way for him…but a lighthouse will never alter its direction no matter what is coming at it. All ships, even battle ships have to alter their direction because of the lighthouse. Jesus is the lighthouse. No matter who we think we are, or how much power we think we have, we can't make Jesus alter His direction to us. We must alter our lives to Jesus. Jesus'

Word is not going to change. You are going to have to change your life to line up with His Word. Jesus is still the only way to heaven. It was that way 2000 years ago, and it will be that way until Jesus comes back. John 14:6 says, *"Jesus answered, I am the way, and the truth and the life. No one comes to the Father except through me."* We need to have a change of heart. We need to be willing to lay down our pride and humble ourselves before Him. It's not about how good, or how strong, or how wise we are. It is about humbly bowing before the King of Kings.

We know the soldiers were not in control of this arrest because they bowed before the One they came to arrest. It is also interesting to see who controlled the conversation. Jesus went out to them, and spoke first. He took control of the conversation from the beginning. Usually when cops go to make an arrest they are in control. They are doing the speaking; telling the other person why they are being arrested. But here we see that the person being arrested is in charge.

Jesus Knew Everything That Was Going To Happen

We need to see that what took place here did not surprise Jesus one bit. He was not thinking, "Oh no, I am in a terrible situation now. How am I going to get out of this? I didn't see this coming." Verse 4 starts out saying, *"Jesus knowing all that was going to happen to him…"* Jesus knew. Jesus, in the flesh, was not all knowing. He only knew what the Father revealed to him. The Bible tells us that Jesus didn't

Jesus' Arrest

know when He would return to the earth. He said that only the Father knows the day and the hour. But God the Father revealed things to Jesus that He needed to know. The Father revealed to Jesus how much He was going to suffer. Jesus knew what was waiting for Him. Jesus said over and over again that He was going to be handed over to the chief priests and be killed. Jesus was not surprised when this big crowd came to arrest Him. He was waiting for them.

Jesus knew what the next day would bring. The insults, people spitting in His face, soldiers hitting Him, being flogged on the back 40 times, the crown of thorns pushed down on His head, carrying His own cross, being nailed to the cross...and just hanging there. Knowing all that, He waited around for this crowd to come and get Him. Jesus could have hidden. He could have left town before they even got there. I don't know about you, but if I knew that I was going to face what Jesus was faced with, I think I would be getting out of town. Jesus was not a victim of bad circumstances. He knew that if He stayed He would be laying down His life. The Romans did not overpower Jesus and kill Him against His will. He willingly laid down His life. Jesus says back in John 10:18, *"No one takes it from me, but I lay it down of my own accord. I have authority to lay it down and authority to take it up again. This command I received from my Father."* The Romans didn't have the power to kill Jesus by their own strength. Jesus willingly surrendered Himself to be a sacrifice for our sins. Jesus was committed to following the Father's will.

Jesus was human, He didn't want to go through that

much suffering. He prayed to His Father, "take this cup from me, but not my will, but yours be done." He was willing to die because there was so much depending on His suffering. Our eternal home rested on the decision whether Jesus would die or not.

Jesus was willing to follow the Father's will, even though He knew it would take Him to the cross. He was willing to do that because He knew His Father and He knew He could trust His Father. He knew His Father was in control. This was not a spur of the moment decision by God. "Well, the people have sinned—what are we going to do now? I guess we are going to have to send Jesus into the world to die." God never lost control. He was in control the whole time. 1 Peter 1:20 says, *"He* (Jesus) *was chosen before the creation of the world, but was revealed in these last times for your sake."* God knew before the creation of the world that He would have to send His Son into the world to die for us. God knew, even before He created us, that we would sin against Him and need Jesus to die for us. Jesus on the cross was not the result of God panicking or God being out of options. It was God proving His love for each and every one of us. Jesus had His way out, He knew ahead of time that danger was on its way. But He chose to stay and die, so that we could have eternal life in heaven.

He Protected His Disciples

When Jesus was arrested He was ready to go and give His life for us. But the disciples still had some fight left in them. After all, Peter had a weapon. Peter grabbed a sword and took off someone's ear. You really can't blame Peter. If I was in that situation I might have done the same thing. I would want to do everything I could to protect Jesus. But Peter did not have the power to protect Jesus. He could have taken out a couple of people here or there, but he had no chance of taking on the whole crowd with all of the weapons they had. Jesus, on the other hand, had the power to defend Himself. He could have called, and legions of angels would have come down to fight for Him. He could have walked out of this terrible situation untouched. But Jesus knew that was not part of the plan. Jesus was not there to save Himself, He was there to save those who follow Him. Jesus wanted to protect His disciples because they were the primary agents who would preach His gospel to the whole world. Verses 8 & 9 say, *"Jesus answered, 'if you are looking for me, then let these men go.' This happened so that the words he had spoken would be fulfilled: I have not lost one of those you gave me."* If the mob had been in control here, the disciples would have been arrested and killed as well. We see this image that Jesus gave us back in John 10, that He is the good shepherd. The good shepherd is willing to lay down His life to protect His flock. That is what Jesus did, He gave Himself to save His followers.

When we come to the arrest, trial and crucifixion of Jesus—sometimes it may look like He has lost control. They arrest Him, beat Him, and kill Him. How can He be in control and let that happen? But Jesus made it very, very clear, "No one takes my life from me, but I lay it down of my own accord."[25] In this passage of scripture, the apostle John who was an eyewitness, wanted to make sure to let us know that Jesus was the one in charge—not the Romans, not the Jewish leaders, not the mob, not the disciples…but Jesus. Jesus was not forced to die for you, He did it willingly out of His great love for you.

I like this passage because sometimes in our lives we may wonder if God is really in control. It doesn't look like it, or it doesn't feel like it. But if you really stop to look at whatever you are going through, you can know that God is in control.

Peter's Denials

There is a movie called "The Three Musketeers." The Musketeers were the king's personal soldiers. They swore to protect the king. In this movie there is an evil advisor trying to take away the kingdom from the king. The evil advisor disbanded the Musketeers, saying that he needed all of them in the regular army because they were about to go to war. But the real reason he disbanded the Musketeers was that he had the regular army under his control and he had a plot to kill the king. With the Musketeers out of the way, it would be easy to kill the king. The evil advisor said to the Musketeers, that they needed to surrender their roles as Musketeers, or they would all be arrested. Because of the threat of being arrested, one by one, people gave up their swords and their cloaks that signified that they were Musketeers. But there were three musketeers who stayed loyal to their king even if the punishment would be prison or death. Would you stay loyal to your king, if your allegiance would mean prison or death?

Jesus has proclaimed Himself as king, but we see that His followers briefly lost their "musketeer" courage. In this chapter, we will be looking at one of Jesus' follower's reaction when he could be facing prison or death for his allegiance to

King Jesus. Before I get into the main passage, I want to start by giving a little background of what took place earlier. Jesus was in the garden with His disciples before He was arrested. In Matthew 26:31 it says, *"Then Jesus told them, This very night you will all fall away on account of me."* Peter responds in verse 33, *"Even if all fall away on account of you, I never will."* Peter is voicing his allegiance to Jesus. But Jesus goes on to say that Peter will deny Him. Peter comes back and tells Jesus how loyal he is to Him. Verse 35, *"But Peter declared, Even if I have to die with you, I will never disown you."* Peter swore that he would never leave his king, no matter if death was waiting for him. Just like the musketeers in the movie. They swore loyalty to their king, but only three musketeers stayed loyal to their king. Let's see if Peter keeps his promise and stays loyal to his king. Matthew 26 tells the story.

> [69] *Now Peter was sitting out in the courtyard, and a servant girl came to him. "You also were with Jesus of Galilee," she said.*
> [70] *But he denied it before them all. "I don't know what you're talking about," he said.*
> [71] *Then he went out to the gateway, where another girl saw him and said to the people there, "This fellow was with Jesus of Nazareth."*
> [72] *He denied it again, with an oath: "I don't know the man!"*
> [73] *After a little while, those standing there went up to Peter and said, "Surely you are one*

of them, for your accent gives you away."

⁷⁴ Then he began to call down curses on himself and he swore to them, "I don't know the man!" Immediately a rooster crowed. ⁷⁵ Then Peter remembered the word Jesus had spoken: "Before the rooster crows, you will disown me three times." And he went outside and wept bitterly.

With the chaos of the arrest, Peter quietly shifted identities. No longer a follower of Jesus, he became one of the crowd, trying to blend in. Jesus was on trial before the Sanhedrin…while you could say, Peter was on trial out in the courtyard. As you look at the denials of Peter, you see a progression as each denial takes place.

The first denial: <u>Peter pleaded ignorance</u>. A servant girl came up to him in the courtyard and said, "You were with Jesus." Notice Peter's response in verse 70, *"But he denied it before them all. I don't know what you're talking about, he said."* Peter is trying to pass this off as nothing. He doesn't want this to become a debate or a long drawn out conversation. He doesn't want the spotlight on him. He wants to brush this off and move on. A servant girl is very low in popularity in this culture, so if he brushes her off, maybe no one will give this servant girl's comment a second thought. So Peter plays ignorant. Peter must be thinking to himself, "Hopefully this will put an end to this."

But then another girl sees him and says that he was with Jesus. <u>Peter's second denial he made with an oath.</u>

Verse 72 says, *"he denied it again, with an oath: I don't know the man!"* Peter bumps his denial up another notch here. The questions are still coming, so he uses more force to squash this talk before a bigger crowd gets involved. So Peter does two things. He drops the ignorance defense and he makes no doubt that he is answering their question. I don't know the man. I don't know this Jesus, you speak of. He also responds by making an oath. An oath in Jewish culture made God a party to the assertion being made. It was a way of calling down the judgment of God if the words spoken were false. Basically Peter is saying, "As God as my witness, I don't know Jesus." In fear, Peter makes God a witness to his lie. Peter, "the rock that Jesus is going to build His church upon", doesn't look much like a rock right now. But it gets even worse.

    The third denial: <u>Peter made an oath & curses</u>. The people didn't believe his first two denials, so Peter has to further intensify his claim of disassociating himself with Jesus. On top of the oaths, "Calling God as his witness that he doesn't know the man", now he calls down curses. There is some disagreement on who is the object of the curses. NIV says that Peter is calling curses down upon himself…where the King James and other versions don't say who Peter is cursing. In the Biblical commentaries that really dig into the Greek language, the thought is that Peter was cursing Jesus. Here is a quote from one of the Greek commentaries. "Most have suggested that Peter cursed himself or the bystanders. But the best guess is that Jesus is the object of the curse; just as persecuted Christians were later asked to curse Jesus and so disassociate themselves from their religion, so Peter here curses Jesus in an attempt to prove that he is not one of his followers." People are really investigating Peter. This is the third time that they are questioning him. Peter has to be sweating this a little bit. "How much longer till they get the authorities involved in this situation and they arrest me." So, in an attempt to convince the people once and for all, he calls down curses, either on himself or Jesus. He emphatically denies any association with Jesus whatsoever.

Intention cannot always be judged by something we do once. Sometimes we just mess up. But Peter didn't just mess up once and then get his act together and recover the second time. Peter repeatedly saved his own hide by disassociating himself with Jesus. Peter was in denial mode all the way. They could have asked him eight times that night…his intention was not to own up to being a follower of Jesus Christ. It's not that Peter didn't have time to stop and reflect on his denials. We are not sure how closely the first two denials happened, but we know that the third denial happened later. In Luke 22:59 it says, *"About an hour later another asserted, "Certainly this fellow was with him, for he is a Galilean."* Peter had at least an hour to stop and process how he denied Jesus two times, but did he even give it much thought, as he was in the middle of it all? Was he less reflective on what he was doing, and more focused on future ways he could hide this from the people? "It doesn't matter that what I'm doing is wrong, I just want to make sure I don't get caught. I don't want other people to know." No matter if we can hide it from other people or not, God knows the truth of our denials. Hebrews 4:13 says, *"Nothing in all of creation is hidden from God's sight. Everything is uncovered and laid bare before the eyes of him to whom we must give account."* He sees it all. Every word and every action. We can't cover it up. We may fool people, but God knows.

In Luke 22:61 it says, (just after his third denial, the rooster crowed,) *"The Lord turned and looked straight at Peter. Then Peter remembered the word the Lord has spoken to him: Before the rooster crows today, you will disown me three times."* Peter blatantly, unashamedly denied Jesus three times and then looked straight into the eyes of Jesus. You talk about your heart breaking. Can you imagine the shame Peter must have felt? Peter looked into Jesus' eyes everyday for three years as he followed Him. He looked straight into the eyes of Jesus when he made his bold confession of faith. Matthew 16:16 says, *"Simon Peter answered, You are the Christ, the Son of the living God."* His spirit inside him is probably full of wonder and excitement that he is looking at the Son of the Living God. But now Peter looks into those same eyes, after convincingly denying even knowing Jesus on 3 separate occasions…oh the shame that he must have felt. Peter was confident in his allegiance to Jesus. It was just hours earlier that Peter boldly proclaimed, "I will never leave you, no matter if I have to die with you." It wasn't months or weeks or even days earlier that Peter insisted that he would never deny Him...it was just a couple of hours earlier. But within those few hours, Peter's world unraveled and he did something that he will always regret. HE DIDN'T STAY FAITHFUL TO JESUS.

Maybe as you are reading this, you can identify with Peter. You proclaim Him as Christ, as the Son of the living God and that you would be willing to follow Him no matter what happens to you. But then come the things that you wish you could take back. The late nights on the computer looking at pictures you shouldn't be looking at. Oh, what if you looked into His eyes at that moment of denial. What shame you would be feeling. Maybe you cheated your neighbor, or gossiped about your co-workers, or the drinking that got out of control, the lusts you couldn't control…Can you imagine the shame Peter felt looking into Jesus eyes?

After Peter denied Him, the rooster crowed three times. Verse 75 says, *"Then Peter remembered the word Jesus had spoken: Before the rooster crows, you will disown me three times." And he went outside and wept bitterly."* Peter left and wept bitterly. This is not a tear coming down his cheek… this is a rip my heart out of my chest, I want to die feeling. The guilt had to be overwhelming. He could not believe what he had done. "Is it possible that I actually did that?" Could he ever find forgiveness for denying his Lord? This would be the longest weekend in Peter's life. This either happened late on Thursday night or very early on Friday morning. Peter had to be replaying over and over again his unfaithfulness. Oh to be able to take that back. There would be no comfort or peace for Peter. He was racked with guilt because he was disloyal to his King.

Can you see how horrible his weekend would be? But that all changed on Sunday night when he saw Jesus alive. Jesus breaks into the room and says PEACE! Ahh…the weight that must have been lifted off of Peter's heart. That is the only thing that could ever bring peace back to Peter. Without Jesus, Peter was sentenced to a life of guilt because he messed up. It is the same way with us. We have messed up and are doomed to live guilt filled lives until we receive the Peace that comes from the risen Lord. Then we, like Peter, can have victory over our guilt and shame. Some of us are living in the past and keep recalling our denials of Jesus. Our unfaithfulness keeps playing over and over again in our minds. We need to have the encounter that Peter had with the Risen Lord. He is the only thing that can bring us peace. You will read more about the peace that we can have in chapter 13.

As you look at this passage of scripture today it may be one we are well too familiar with in our lives. I am like Peter. I have failed and messed up horribly. Luckily, Jesus is there to offer us His forgiveness. Jesus knew ahead of time that Peter would deny Him. He predicted that it would happen. He wasn't surprised that Peter messed up, and He isn't surprised when you blow it. He was willing and wanting to forgive Peter. And He holds out His hand, ready to forgive you today. 1 John 1:9 says, *"If we confess our sins, he is faithful and just and will forgive us our sins and purify us from all unrighteousness."* We don't serve a God who is waiting for us to mess up so that He can take away His love for us. We serve a compassionate God who holds out His hands to sin-prone individuals. John Newton, the hymn writer of Amazing Grace once said, "I am getting old and my memory is nearly gone, but two things I remember. One, I am a wretched sinner, and two, Jesus is a great savior."

As you finish this chapter, are you truly sorry for the times you have denied Jesus in your life? If so, read on and you will know the peace the Risen Christ came to give you.

THE TRIAL

I would like to share with you a story about five blind men. None of them had ever encountered an elephant before, and they wondered what it looked like. So each of them was lead to the elephant. The first one reached out and touched the elephant and he touched its side. It was long and sturdy—so the man thought to himself that the elephant looked like a wall. The second man went up and felt the elephant's tusk. It was round, long and smooth, and it had a sharp end—so he thought for sure the elephant looked like a spear. The third man approached the elephant and felt its trunk. It was long and squirmy—He said anybody can tell that an elephant is like a snake. The fourth man went and touched the elephant's leg. He felt up and down—it is obvious that an elephant looks like a tree. The fifth man went up and touched the elephant's tail. It was skinny and long—He said the elephant must look like a jump rope. All five of these men encountered the elephant... All five of these men thought they <u>knew the truth</u> about what the elephant looked like. These five men argued back and forth, each thinking they knew the truth. The truth was right in front of them, but the problem was that they jumped to conclusions. Each of these five men only knew one part of the truth—and it distorted their view of the whole elephant.[26]

In this chapter we are going to see two people who didn't see the truth about Jesus even when they were right in front of Him. They jumped to conclusions about who He was. In John 18, Jesus finally came straight out and told us exactly who He is...He is king!

> [28] *Then the Jews led Jesus from Caiaphas to the palace of the Roman governor. By now it was early morning, and to avoid ceremonial uncleanness the Jews did not enter the palace; they wanted to be able to eat the Passover.* [29] *So Pilate came out to them and asked, "What charges are you bringing against this man?"*
> [30] *"If he were not a criminal," they replied, "we would not have handed him over to you."*
> [31] *Pilate said, "Take him yourselves and judge him by your own law."*
> *"But we have no right to execute anyone," the Jews objected.* [32] *This happened so that the words Jesus had spoken indicating the kind of death he was going to die would be fulfilled.*
> [33] *Pilate then went back inside the palace, summoned Jesus and asked him, "Are you the king of the Jews?"*
> [34] *"Is that your own idea," Jesus asked, "or did others talk to you about me?"*
> [35] *"Am I a Jew?" Pilate replied. "It was your people and your chief priests who handed you over to me. What is it you have done?"*

36 Jesus said, "My kingdom is not of this world. If it were, my servants would fight to prevent my arrest by the Jews. But now my kingdom is from another place."

37 "You are a king, then!" said Pilate.

Jesus answered, "You are right in saying I am a king. In fact, for this reason I was born, and for this I came into the world, to testify to the truth. Everyone on the side of truth listens to me."

38 "What is truth?" Pilate asked. With this he went out again to the Jews and said, "I find no basis for a charge against him. 39 But it is your custom for me to release to you one prisoner at the time of the Passover. Do you want me to release 'the king of the Jews'?"

40 They shouted back, "No, not him! Give us Barabbas!" Now Barabbas had taken part in a rebellion.

The Jews Were Not Interested In The Truth

The Jewish leaders wanted Jesus dead. They were jealous of Jesus because they were the religious leaders of the day, then Jesus came along and everyone started to follow Him. These Jewish leaders gave Jesus a mock trial, but they were not interested in the truth. They knew exactly how they were going to judge Him from the beginning of the trial. They wouldn't even listen—they had their opinion about who He was and nothing was going to change their opinion of Him. They found Jesus guilty and they took Him to the Roman government to be judged. They brought Him before Pilate who was the Roman governor. Pilate met them and asked them in verse 29, *"What charges are you bringing against this man."* This is a normal question at the beginning of a trial. Pilate needed to know the charges before he could hear the case. But the problem was that the Jewish leaders didn't have any kind of charge against Jesus that would stand up in Roman court. Jesus never killed anyone. He didn't steal anything from anyone. These Jewish leaders didn't have a very strong case to bring to Pilate. Their only response to Pilate was in verse 30, *"If he were not a criminal, we would not have handed him over to you."* Jesus didn't do anything wrong, but they wanted Him dead.

Pilate understood that they claimed Jesus broke one of their religious laws—and he didn't want to get involved in their religious disputes, so he said, "Judge Him yourself with your own laws." But that would not do for the Jews. They wanted Jesus to be killed, and they wanted the Romans to do it. Verse 31-32 says, *"Pilate said, take him yourselves and judge him by your own law. But we have no right to execute anyone, the Jews objected. This happened so that the words Jesus had spoken indicating the kind of death he was going to die would be fulfilled."* The Roman Government was the power in charge of Israel at this time. That is why the Jews went to them to get Jesus executed. However, the Jews sometimes carried out the death penalty on their own. In John chapter 8 we read about a woman caught in the act of adultery, and the Jews wanted to stone her. Also in the book of Acts we read about the Jews stoning Stephen, one of Jesus' followers. When the Jews took upon themselves to execute someone, they would stone them. They would pick up huge stones and throw them at the person. So why didn't they take Jesus out back and stone Him without the Romans. Well again, we see that Jesus is in charge. Jesus predicted that His death would be by the Romans and not by the Jews. In John 12:32, Jesus says *"But I, when I am lifted up from the earth, will draw all men to myself."* In this passage He was talking to His disciples about His upcoming death. He was going to be lifted up. To be lifted up, means to be lifted up unto a cross. Only the Romans carried out the capital offense by hanging people on crosses. Jesus said, When I am lifted up—when I die on the cross—I will draw all men to myself. Because I go to the cross, salvation is possible for all. The cross draws us to God. Jesus knew His death would be on a cross and that it would bring people to God.

The Jews wanted Jesus dead at any cost, so they gave Him a mock trial. Could you imagine being a part of a trial where people have already made up their mind about the verdict? "I would like to call my first witness." "Don't bother, we already think that he is guilty." "But he is an eye witness that saw the whole thing." "Don't want to hear about it…he is guilty and nothing, no matter how much evidence you have, will change my mind." Can you believe that would ever take place? Well, there are many people in our world who believe that they know the truth about God without even doing any investigation whatsoever. I'm not going to go to church; I am not going to read the Bible—because I know that He is not God; what a waste of time. They jump to conclusions before looking at all of the evidence. The Bible has a lot to say. Maybe you believe it, maybe not… but hopefully you read it first before you made up your mind. There is a lot at stake. You will either spend eternity in the perfect place of heaven, or you will face eternal punishment in hell. With that at stake, I would suggest that you at least read it (look at all the evidence) before you cast your verdict, your eternal verdict on your soul.

Pilate Was Blinded To The Truth

The Jews brought Jesus to Pilate to be judged. The only charge that could really be held against Jesus would be if He claimed to be a king. If Jesus claimed to be a king, He would be guilty of treason. In Roman jurisdiction, there was only one King…and that was Caesar. So Pilate had to figure out whether Jesus claimed to be king or not. Let's read verses 36-38. *"Jesus said, 'My kingdom is not of this world. If it were, my servants would fight to prevent my arrest by the Jews. But now my kingdom is from another place.' 'You are a king, then!' said Pilate. Jesus answered, 'You are right in saying I am a king. In fact, for this reason I was born, and for this I came into the world, to testify to the truth. Everyone on the side of truth listens to me.' 'What is truth?' Pilate asked."* Jesus tells Pilate very clearly, "I am a king." His kingdom is not of this world. So why did Jesus leave His kingdom? We get the answer right here in verse 37. *"For this reason I was born, and for this I came into the world."* The reason...to testify to the truth. People needed to know the truth. Jesus left His heavenly palace, His heavenly kingdom—to show us the truth. He finishes verse 37 by saying *"Everyone on the side of truth listens to me."* Jesus is saying, "Those who have truth in them will follow me. They will recognize the voice of truth." Do you hear that: they will recognize the voice of truth. Pilate immediately says, *"What is truth?"* He doesn't recognize the truth when it is standing right there in front of him.

What is the truth? It is a question that people ask today. We see in today's society that "truth" is whatever you want it to be. Truth varies from person to person. But the fact is that there are absolute truths that are true for all of us. Two plus two is always four. It is not three on some days, and four on other days. It is not six, just because you want it to be six. The truth is the truth no matter if you believe it or not. Just because you think two plus two is five and you convince other people of the same thing, doesn't make it right. Truth is truth even when you choose not to believe it. Jesus tells us in John 14:6, *"I am the way and the truth and the life. No one comes to the Father except through me."* Jesus doesn't say I have truth. Some little part of me is truth—I have the truth quality in me. No, Jesus is saying I AM truth. Pilate was face to face with the truth, and he asks, "What is truth—I don't understand." Then he turned his back to the truth and walked out of the room.

Maybe we are like Pilate with the truth. We go to church and hear the truth, but it doesn't stick with us because we are more interested in other things. We go to church to make our spouses happy…maybe bring a little contentment to our conscience. But we are not truly seeking the truth because the truth may complicate our lifestyle. If I realize the truth, how I view life has to change. I don't get to dictate what truth is anymore. If Pilate saw Jesus as the truth, Pilate would have to question his life and the power and position that he had. And if you saw Jesus as the truth, what changes would that make for your life? "I would have to give up the drinking I like to do, I would have to give up all my lustful additions—inappropriate movies and computer images…if I saw Jesus as the truth—I couldn't be the self centered person I want to be. There is a standard I am supposed to live by." People like Pilate are not open to the truth because they know that it will change their lives.

Pilate wasn't against Jesus in this passage. He even tried to free Jesus. Pilate said in verse 38, *"I find no basis for a charge against him."* Pilate said, I find nothing wrong in Him. So why did he crucify Him and not stand up for Him? Pilate cared more about his job and keeping the peace in Jerusalem than he did about the truth. Too many churchgoers are like Pilate. They are not against Jesus, they will come and listen to Jesus' word being spoken…but when the rubber meets the road, the truth will take second place to the things that are going to benefit them. There may be some people reading this that go to church every week to hear the truth, but it doesn't change how they live.

Will You Reject The Truth?

After Pilate completed his investigation of Jesus, he came out to the crowd and said, "I find no basis for a charge against Him." I think He is innocent, now it is up to you. Pilate even calls Him a king in verse 39. *"Do you want me to release the king of the Jews?"* But the crowd wanted him to release Barabbas. They rejected the king that came to save them. We are faced with the same decision that the crowd had that day. We must decide whether we believe that Jesus is who He says He is. There is no way of misinterpreting Jesus...He comes flat out and says that He is a king. If we say that He is a king—He needs to become the king of our lives.

Again I would like to look at verse 36, *"Jesus said, My kingdom is not of this world. If it were, my servants would fight to prevent my arrest by the Jews. But now my kingdom is from another place."* His kingdom is not of this world. So if we are followers of Him, we are not in our kingdom. This world is not our home. We should not be at home in this world, because we are foreigners. As Paul says in Philippians 3:20, *"But our citizenship is in heaven. And we eagerly await a Savior from there, the Lord Jesus Christ..."* We are citizens of heaven, we are just passing through. Can people tell that you are a citizen of heaven and that Jesus is your king?

A missionary tells a story about how there were no national boundaries between countries, so the people of Laos and the people of Vietnam started to build houses in the same communities. This made it very difficult for the kings to know how to tax their people because they were mixed in with people from another country. So the kings came to an agreement. Those who ate short-grain rice, built their houses on stilts, and decorated them with Indian-style serpents were considered Laotians. On the other hand, those who ate long-grain rice, built their houses on the ground, and decorated them with Chinese-style dragons were considered Vietnamese. The exact location of a person's home was not what determined his or her nationality. Instead, each person belonged to the kingdom whose cultural values he or she exhibited.[27] So it is with us: we are mixed in with the people of the world. Can people see by our values that we are citizens of heaven?

The sad point in this passage is that there was not one person willing to stand up for Jesus and say, "Jesus is the truth—and He is my king." There was not a hunger for truth in this passage. But Praise the Lord, I know that there is still a hunger for the truth in this world today. Not too long ago several people said to me, "We don't know very much about the Bible—and we want to know more—can we meet during the week to ask you questions? God is stirring in people's hearts. There is a hunger for more of God's Word. Keep seeking truth from His Word. Matthew 5:6 says, *"Blessed are those who hunger and thirst for righteousness, for they will be filled."* If you confess that Jesus is truth, and you desire to know more about Him…God will reveal Himself to you.

Humble King To Conquering King

THE CROSS

We have all heard the story many times...Jesus died on the cross, was laid in a tomb, and rose again on the third day. We have heard it so much that maybe it has lost its sense of wonder. It has become just a story to us.

Well there was a Good Friday service in Bangladesh, and it was packed. Many people who had never heard the message of Jesus attended the service. They were there to see a movie about Jesus' life. Little children sat on the floor in the aisles and across the front of the church. Rows of people stood in the back. They saw the love of Jesus come through the film—He healed people, taught them, and cared about the people who came to Him. The people who watched the movie drew close to Jesus by just watching His life. But then came the crucifixion scene. People were weeping and gasping in unbelief. They couldn't believe what was happening to Jesus. As they watched, they were feeling the agony of Jesus' pain...and they felt the disappointment of the disciples. In that emotional moment, a young boy in the crowd, couldn't stand it any longer, and he cried out, "Don't worry. I have seen the movie before. He gets up again."[28] Have we lost that sense of astonishment that Jesus would actually die on the cross for us? Have we lost the great sense of joy that Jesus rose from the dead?

It can be easy to think about the Holy week and to be nonchalant about the whole thing...because we know the whole story. We know that Jesus did rise from the dead on Sunday morning. But can you imagine what the disciples must have been feeling as this week unfolded? Thursday night they would be celebrating the Passover with their Lord, eating and drinking, singing hymns—not knowing that in a couple of hours—Jesus would be arrested. Friday night comes and they are sitting in the dark, wondering "How can this be? How could Jesus be dead?" There was no hope in their spirits that He would be raised to life again...they were locked in a room, scared to leave. Can you see the sense of hopelessness that they must have been feeling? They needed someone like the little boy in the opening story to come along and say, "Wait, that's not the end...He will rise again." And that is what the prophet Isaiah did hundreds of years before it even happened. Isaiah 52:13- 53:7 predicted this event.

> [13] *See, my servant will act wisely; he will be raised and lifted up and highly exalted.*
> [14] *Just as there were many who were appalled at him—his appearance was so disfigured beyond that of any man and his form marred beyond human likeness—*
> [15] *so will he sprinkle many nations, and kings will shut their mouths because of him.*
> *For what they were not told, they will*

see, and what they have not heard, they will understand.

Who has believed our message and to whom has the arm of the LORD been revealed?

² He grew up before him like a tender shoot, and like a root out of dry ground.

He had no beauty or majesty to attract us to him, nothing in his appearance that we should desire him.

³ He was despised and rejected by men, a man of sorrows, and familiar with suffering.

Like one from whom men hide their faces he was despised, and we esteemed him not.

⁴ Surely he took up our infirmities and carried our sorrows, yet we considered him stricken by God, smitten by him, and afflicted.

⁵ But he was pierced for our transgressions, he was crushed for our iniquities; the punishment that brought us peace was upon him, and by his wounds we are healed.

⁶ We all, like sheep, have gone astray, each of us has turned to his own way; and the LORD has laid on him the iniquity of us all.

⁷ He was oppressed and afflicted, yet he did not open his mouth; he was led like a lamb to the slaughter, and as a sheep before her shearers is silent, so he did not open his mouth.

The Messiah Who Would Come And Rescue God's People

Isaiah tells us that a Messiah will come and rescue God's people, but he doesn't tell us what the Messiah will look like. Not even one physical characteristic. There are many pictures of Jesus. All of them capture about the same things…beard, long hair, and other details you can get from these pictures. But we have no idea what He looked like. The Bible doesn't give us the first description of Jesus' appearance. The Bible tells us a lot about other people's appearance, but not a word about Jesus. We know some people were left-handed, some were handsome, some were heavy set, some had long hair. There was Esau who was red and hairy, Zacchaeus who was short, and Goliath who was tall. We know a little bit about a couple of the great kings in the Old Testament. The first king in Israel's history, King Saul, was a big man—he stood a head taller than anybody else. People were willing to follow a strong, powerful guy like that. He looked kingly. The Bible describes King Absalom as the most handsome in all Israel—people are willing to follow someone who looks like a king, someone who looks royal. There were many other people described by their looks. Why wouldn't they share about Jesus' appearance? He is the most important person in the Bible.

What does the Bible say about Jesus? The only description we get of Jesus is a prophecy that happened over 400 years before He was born. Isaiah didn't proclaim that there would be a handsome, tall, strong man who was going to save you. Isaiah never saw Jesus, but this is what was revealed to him by the Spirit of God. Isaiah says in Isaiah 53:2, *"He had no beauty or majesty to attract us to him, nothing in his appearance that we should desire him."* He is ordinary. He doesn't look like royalty. It was not His appearance that drew people to Him. Jesus never dressed like a king. Only once did He walk around in His glory. When no crowd was around, He was on a mountain with only three of His disciples—He transformed before their eyes. His clothes became as bright as lightning, His face shone like the sun. The disciples were in awe. A huge cloud surrounded them—and then when the cloud cleared—there was "regular ole Jesus." Let me tell you, if people were around and saw that, if they would have seen Jesus in His glory, if Jesus would have walked around daily with His face shining like the sun and His clothes as bright as lightning—people would have seen the King that He was. But Jesus didn't walk around like that; He even told His disciples not to tell anyone what they saw until He rose from the dead.

This verse in Isaiah said that Jesus had nothing in His appearance to attract us to Him. That is because in Philippians 2 it says, *"Jesus emptied himself."* When Jesus left heaven, He set aside His glory. He became one of us, there was nothing in Jesus' earthly appearance that made people gravitate toward Him. It was His compassion, His mercy, His love…that brought thousands to His side. We don't need to know what Jesus looked like. All we need to know is the love He has for all who come to Him.

The Reason Jesus Would Go To The Cross

Verse 6 explains why this Servant of God must suffer. *"We all, like sheep, have gone astray, each of us has turned to his own way; and the Lord has laid on him the iniquity of us all."* Because we turned away…Jesus carried our sins. He is the only one who could.

A distressed father sat at the bedside of his comatose son who was hurt playing basketball. At a crucial point in the game, the 16-year-old lunged for an errant pass going out of bounds. As he toppled over a spectator's chair, one of its legs caught him in the stomach and damaged vital organs. Because he felt little pain, the teen continued to play the game's final minutes while he hemorrhaged internally. By the time the pain grew enough to warrant a trip to the hospital, it was almost too late. The doctors worked frantically to save him, but the outcome was uncertain. Though the son eventually recovered, those awful hours of waiting for the slightest signs of recovery forced family members to ask questions they'd never before faced. The father was alone on his bedside shift one evening when the pastor visited. Trembling with emotion, the father asked, "Will God kill my son to punish my sin?" "No," said the young minister, searching for words that would comfort and grant renewed trust in the God this father now so desperately needed. "The Lord's not punishing *your* son for your sin. He can't, because God punished *his* son for your sin."[29]

Jesus was punished for your sins. The Lord laid on Jesus the iniquity of us all. Jesus bore the sin of the world. Jesus took God's wrath that was meant for you and endured it for your sake. Verse 4, *"Surely he took up our infirmities and carried our sorrows, yet we considered him stricken by God, smitten by him, and afflicted."* He took our sins and sorrows and He unselfishly went to the cross. But there were some people who said, "He is getting what he deserves." They gathered around the cross and could not see what He was doing for them. They just sat back and thought, God is giving this blasphemer what He deserves. God is punishing Him because He claims to be equal to Him. There are many people today who are the same way. When they look at what Jesus did, they don't see it as "Jesus did this for me." They may not think Jesus deserved death, but they can't comprehend that they need His sacrifice. This is something He didn't have to do. He could have just spoken a word or shown some of His power…He would have been whisked away back to His glory. But He didn't say a word. Like sheep lead to the slaughter, He was quiet and endured the suffering. Jesus could have made a persuasive argument to Pilate and been released and not had to face the cross. Pilate begged Jesus to speak in His defense so that he didn't have to kill Him. But

Jesus knew that He had to be the sacrifice that would bring healing upon us. So He kept silent and was led away to die.

Mark 15:29-32 tells us the mocking that Jesus received as He was on the cross. *"Those who passed by hurled insults at him, shaking their heads and saying, 'So! You who are going to destroy the temple and build it in three days, come down from the cross and save yourself!' In the same way the chief priests and the teachers of the law mocked him among themselves. 'He saved others,' they said, 'but he can't save himself! ³² Let this Christ, this King of Israel, come down now from the cross, that we may see and believe.' Those crucified with him also heaped insults on him."* How hard it must have been for Jesus to remain silent and not prove Himself. If it had been me on that cross and people were saying things like that, I would have proven to them that I could come down off of that cross. Yet Jesus took their abuse and did not try to prove Himself to them. Jesus could have proved beyond a shadow of a doubt that He was the Christ by coming off of that cross, but we would have still been dead in our sins. The reason He came was to hang on that cross. So Isaiah says, *"He was oppressed and afflicted, yet he did not open his mouth."*

This Isaiah passage tells us how bad the cross would be for Jesus. I have seen many Jesus movies. Most Jesus movies water down His suffering a little bit. They show Him getting beat with whips, then show lines on His back. But if any of you saw the movie "Passion of the Christ" you saw a totally different perspective. Jesus didn't just have lines on His back. It was very graphic…He had skin coming off of

Him—there was no part of Him that was not bloody. That image has stuck with me. You read what Isaiah says in this passage, 52:14, *"Just as there were many who were appalled at him—his appearance was so disfigured beyond that of any man and his form marred beyond human likeness."* His appearance was so disfigured! After Jesus' arrest, He was beaten the whole time until the cross. The Jews hit Him and spit on Him during the trial. They took Him to the Romans and they hit Him, they whipped Him 39 times, and put a crown of thorns on His head. Jesus endured some serious suffering, they made Him carry the weight of the cross to His own execution, they nailed His hands & feet to the cross. Verse 5 uses words to show how bad the cross was. He was <u>pierced</u>. He was <u>crushed</u>. The punishment that brought us peace was upon Him and by His wounds we are healed. Because He was crushed and pierced, we can have peace in our souls, eternal peace with God. God took His wrath that we deserved and He placed it upon His Son. We cannot comprehend the suffering that Jesus had to go through—and we cannot comprehend the benefits that we received from that suffering.

Isaiah Also Predicts The Resurrection

Isaiah does point to the fact that the Messiah will be raised to life again. I will be brief on this point because Part 3 talks more in-depth about the resurrection. The servant of God is going to be slaughtered like a lamb to save us from sin, but He will rise again. Even 400 years before His death took place Isaiah predicts that He would live again. There is a lot of talk about resurrection in Isaiah 53: 10-12. But verse 11 comes right out and says there will be a resurrection, *"After the suffering of his soul, he will see the light of life and be satisfied."* He will see life…He will live again. We can see Isaiah is clearly pointing to Jesus' cruel death on the cross and His resurrection.

The disciples didn't know that He was going to be raised. We do. The disciples didn't know the peace with God that the cross would bring. We do. The disciples lived in despair. We don't. This was a dark Friday for the disciples because of the grief and confusion. Yet today we look at the same day and we call it "<u>Good</u> Friday." We see the cross, as painful as it was for Jesus, but we understand that it was the greatest thing that could happen for mankind.

Actor Kevin Bacon recounted when his 6-year-old son saw one of his movies for the first time. This is how the conversation went: He said, "Hey, Dad, you know that thing in the movie where you swing from the rafters of that building? That's really cool, how did you do that?" I said, "Well, I didn't do that part--it was a stunt man." "What's a stunt man?" he asked. "That's someone who dresses like me and does things I can't do." "Oh," he replied and walked out of the room looking a little confused. A little later he said, "Hey, Dad, you know that thing in the movie where you spin around on that gym bar and land on your feet? How did you do that?" I said, "Well, I didn't do that. It was a gymnastics double." "What's a gymnastics double?" he asked. "That's a guy who dresses in my clothes and does things I can't do." There was silence from my son, then he asked in a concerned voice, "Dad, what did you do?" I said sheepishly, "I got all the glory." YOU KNOW…That's the grace of God in our lives. Jesus was our stunt double… Jesus did what we couldn't do. And we stand forgiven and bask sheepishly, triumphant in Jesus' glory. He did the work, and we get to bask in His glory.[30]

Humble King To Conquering King

PART 3

THE RISEN KING

For we know that since Christ was raised from the dead, he cannot die again; death no longer has mastery over him.

Romans 6:9

Humble King To Conquering King

THE EMPTY TOMB

There was a minister who returned to his pulpit ten days after his son committed suicide. He choked back the tears as he read Romans 8:28: *"And we know that in all things God works for the good of those who love him, who have been called according to his purpose."* Visibly struggling, he said, "I cannot make my son's suicide fit into this passage. It's impossible for me to see how anything good can come out of it. Yet I realize that I only see in part. I only know in part. "It's like the miracle of the shipyard. Almost every part of our great oceangoing vessels are made of steel. If you take any single part, be it a steel plate out of the hull or the huge rudder, and throw it into the ocean, it will sink. Steel doesn't float! But when the shipbuilders are finished, when the last plate has been riveted in place, then that massive steel ship is virtually unsinkable. "Taken by itself, my son's suicide is senseless. Throw it into the sea of Romans 8:28, and it sinks. Still, I believe that when the Eternal Shipbuilder has finally finished, when God has worked out His perfect design, even this senseless tragedy will somehow work to our eternal good."[31]

That confusion and pain that the pastor was feeling is what the disciples felt in the days between the cross and the resurrection. How could anything good come from the cross? This isolated event was the saddest event in history. But when you finish the story with the resurrection…it is the most powerful, life changing event in all of history. The disciples' world completely changed when they encountered the Risen Christ. As you read this, you may be filled with hurts and pains, or confusion and doubts because of what is happening in our world today, or because of things happening in your life. Well, your entire outlook can change if you truly catch a glimpse of the resurrection of Christ and how it affects your temporary circumstances.

It is helpful to remember the kind of weekend that the disciples and the woman who followed Jesus had had. This man, who they had followed around for the last three years, this man who they had placed all of their hopes in… was gone—dead. Just like that their lives had lost meaning. Thursday night they had been partying at the Passover Feast, and then on Friday they had been grieving at the cross. Confused and crushed with grief they had stayed inside all weekend trying to sort everything out. They have had enough surprises, enough drama for one weekend. But they were about ready to get on the emotional roller coaster one more time. Luke 24 tells us what happens next.

> [1] *On the first day of the week, very early in the morning, the women took the spices they had prepared and went to the tomb.*
> [2] *They found the stone rolled away from the tomb,*

The Empty Tomb

³ but when they entered, they did not find the body of the Lord Jesus.

⁴ While they were wondering about this, suddenly two men in clothes that gleamed like lightning stood beside them.

⁵ In their fright the women bowed down with their faces to the ground, but the men said to them, "Why do you look for the living among the dead?

⁶ He is not here; he has risen! Remember how he told you, while he was still with you in Galilee:

⁷ 'The Son of Man must be delivered into the hands of sinful men, be crucified and on the third day be raised again.'"

⁸ Then they remembered his words.

⁹ When they came back from the tomb, they told all these things to the Eleven and to all the others.

¹⁰ It was Mary Magdalene, Joanna, Mary the mother of James, and the others with them who told this to the apostles.

¹¹ But they did not believe the women, because their words seemed to them like nonsense.

¹² Peter, however, got up and ran to the tomb. Bending over, he saw the strips of linen lying by themselves, and he went away, wondering to himself what had happened.

The Women Remembered The Words Of Jesus

These women were sincere, devoted followers of Jesus. They were not part-time followers. They didn't follow Jesus only when they had time or when they didn't have something else to worry about. They were the last ones at the cross when He was crucified, and they were the first ones to the tomb. They came to the tomb to anoint Jesus' body with spices—<u>fully expecting Him to be there</u>. They didn't wake up that day wondering, "I wonder if Jesus is alive yet." No, they had spices in hand to anoint Jesus' dead body. There was no expectation at all that they would ever see Jesus alive again.

Even though the resurrection had already happened, the women and the disciples' thought process was still in the past. They had pre-resurrection thinking. Their way of thinking and understanding was that Jesus was still dead and in the tomb. Even though He predicted many times that He was going to be raised from the dead on the third day—They really didn't believe it. Jesus spoke in parables often, maybe they thought He was speaking to them figuratively and not literally. He was going to rise from the dead, what did He mean by that? No one really believed that Jesus was physically going to live again. We can look back on it and question them. How can you not believe Jesus would be raised from the dead? But hindsight is 20/20. We live on this side of the empty tomb, while they were living in the heartache of the moment.

In Mark 16:3 we read about the women's problem.

"And they asked each other, who will roll the stone away from the entrance of the tomb?" The stone in front of the tomb is too heavy for these women to move. They didn't know it yet, but that was an irrelevant problem. <u>The resurrection took care of the problem.</u> The fact is the stone was already rolled away. I mention this because we often get caught up in irrelevant problems in our lives. We focus on our problems and not on the empty tomb. We let the problems we face weigh us down so much, and we begin to think it is up to us to move the stone away. But the resurrection takes care of our problems. God still moves stones today! We don't serve a dead God where we are expected to move the stone away on our own. Our God is alive. We need to realign our thoughts and look at our problems against the back drop of the resurrection. Too often we have the same thoughts the women did, pre-resurrection thoughts. We can't handle this problem—this is too much for us. You're right, it would be, if our God were still dead and in the tomb. But He is alive, and our problems are not too big for Him.

The women got to the tomb and it was empty. Can you imagine what must have been running through their minds? Is this the right tomb? Who would have moved His body? You notice their first instinct was not that He was risen! The Bible says that the women were wondering what happened when two angels appeared to them and said, *"Why do you look for the living among the dead? He is not here; he has risen! Remember how he told you, while he was still with you in Galilee; The son of Man must be delivered into the hands of sinful men, be crucified and on the third day be raised to life."* After they heard what the angel said, verse 8 tells us that. *"They remembered his words."* The women believed at that point that Jesus was alive. They didn't need to see Him. They just needed to be reminded of what Jesus said. Jesus said many times in His life that He would be mistreated and killed…but that He would rise on the third day. The women believed that God's Word was coming to pass. They believed that God does not lie and He said that He would do this, so they believed it had happened. Then the women ran off to tell the disciples the great news. They had faith to believe it without seeing Him with their own eyes.

As we go through this life, it can be hard. In our lives we witness hopelessness in the extreme challenges that we face and we can see no answer whatsoever. We need to be like the women; we need to be reminded of Jesus' words. They saw an empty tomb, but they still had hopeless thoughts until they remembered Jesus' words. As you stand in your emptiness, remember Jesus' words. There will be many times in our lives when we will need to remember the things that Jesus has told us. John 16:33 says, *"I have told you these things, so that in me you may have peace. In this world you will have trouble. But take heart! I have overcome the world."* As you stand in a spot filled with emptiness—remember Jesus' words. He has conquered death, He has conquered this world. Emptiness is replaced with life.

The Disciples Were Skeptical Of The Resurrection

It is difficult to believe that someone could come back to life. It just doesn't happen. A letter came from Health and Human Services to a resident of Greenville County, South Carolina that said: "Your food stamps will be stopped, effective March 1992, because we received notice that you passed away. May God bless you. You may reapply if your circumstances change."[32] If your circumstances change? It basically says if you are raised to life you may reapply for food stamps. That seems like a silly letter to most of us... No one is going to come back from the dead to claim food stamps.

Would you believe it if someone told you that they knew a guy who had been dead for a couple of days and that he had risen from the dead? That would be hard to believe. The disciples just couldn't believe it either when the women told them that Jesus had risen from the dead. Verse 11 says, *"But they did not believe the women, because their words <u>seemed</u> to them like nonsense."* It just sounded too illogical to believe. A person who was dead for days, coming back to life again? It would be easy to be skeptical if you were in their position. There are times when it is hard to believe that something is true.

For instance, in 1993 FBI agents conducted a raid of Southwood psychiatric hospital in San Diego, which was under investigation for medical insurance fraud. After hours of reviewing medical records, the agents had worked up an appetite. The agent in charge of the investigation called a nearby pizza parlor to order a quick dinner for his colleagues.

Agent: Hello. I would like to order 10 large pizzas and 40 cans of soda. Pizza Man: And where would you like them delivered? Agent: We're over at the psychiatric hospital. Pizza Man: The psychiatric hospital? Agent: That's right. I'm an FBI agent. Pizza Man: You're an FBI agent? Agent: That's correct. Pizza Man: And you're at the psychiatric hospital? Agent: That's correct. And make sure you don't go through the front doors. We have them locked. You will have to go around to the back to the service entrance to deliver the pizzas. Pizza Man: And you say you're with the FBI? Agent: That's right. How soon can you have the pizza here? Pizza Man: I don't think so… and he hung up the phone.[33]

It just doesn't seem possible or logical. There is no way I can believe this. If anybody should have believed in the resurrection, you would think that it would have been the disciples…they had been following Jesus for three years. They had seen miracle after miracle. Think about all that they saw Jesus do. They saw Jesus feed 5000 men with five loaves of bread and two fish, they saw Jesus calm the sea during a storm, they saw Jesus heal the blind man, they even saw Jesus bring back three people from the dead…but could He raise Himself back from the dead? That is a question they didn't feel confident in answering. To their reasoning, Jesus was a powerful guy, but He was swallowed up by death like every other man.

The disciples, these men of faith, were the very first people to be skeptical about the resurrection. There are a lot of people in the world today that are skeptical of the resurrection, but remember the disciples were the first ones. The resurrection is the heart of our faith—and our early church fathers were slow to accept it. Without the resurrection, our faith is useless. To be a Christian you have to believe that Jesus conquered death, because if He is still in the grave, then there is no way we will ever escape the grave.

Even though the disciples had the testimony of the women, they refused to believe that it had happened. They also went to see the empty tomb and saw the evidence all around it. Yet they still had trouble believing that Jesus actually had risen from the dead. Verse 12 says, *"Peter, however, got up and ran to the tomb. Bending over, he saw the strips of linen lying by themselves, and he went away, wondering to himself what had happened."* They didn't just take a Sunday walk out to the tomb…they ran to the tomb. They wanted some answers or clues to what had happened to Jesus. They looked around and took it all in. They saw, according to John 20:7 *"the cloth was folded up by itself, separated from the linen."* Jesus' grave clothes were folded up neatly. If someone had stolen the body out of the tomb you would think that they would have taken the body in the grave clothes. Why take the time to take off the grave clothes? If they did take the grave clothes off you would think that they would just throw them on the floor and get out of there. But these robbers must not have been in a hurry because they stopped, and took the time to take the clothes off and fold them. Can you imagine that?

A couple of robbers break into your house, and when you get back you don't have a stereo or a TV, but the laundry you left on your bed is folded! That wouldn't happen. If people came to rob Jesus' body out of the tomb, those grave clothes would not be folded nicely.

When they saw the empty tomb and the empty grave clothes, they didn't think, "Praise God, Jesus did actually rise from the dead!" They didn't jump up and down and celebrate the victory that they had in Jesus' resurrection. They didn't do that because they didn't believe it. Verse 12 says "they went away wondering what had happened." Did someone steal his body? Did someone move it to another tomb?

Why didn't their thought process lead them to the decision that Jesus had risen? I am sure it was because the situation that they were in seemed overwhelming. Why are we not jumping up and down and praising God for the victory over sin and death? Is it because logically it is too hard to believe? The circumstances in our lives just seem too overwhelming to believe that Jesus actually conquered anything on our behalf. We lose sight of the resurrection because we are looking at financial ruin. We lose sight of the resurrection because of broken relationships that we were really hoping would work out for us. We lose sight of the resurrection because life has just been overwhelming us. How can I jump up and down while emotionally I feel like I have been conquered? Life has conquered me! I stand at the empty tomb, but I still see death. Where did things go wrong in my life?

We need to change our viewpoint. If the disciples had

known that Jesus rose from the dead, there would have been some serious celebration around the empty tomb. It would have shattered the hopelessness that they were feeling. If we can allow ourselves to believe in the resurrection and see what it has truly done for us—it will shatter the hopelessness we are facing in our lives right now. <u>Everything that we face in this life is temporary…the resurrection is eternal.</u> 2 Corinthians 4:16-18, *"Therefore we do not lose heart. Though outwardly we are wasting away, yet inwardly we are being renewed day by day. For our light and momentary troubles are achieving for us an eternal glory that far outweighs them all. So we fix our eyes not on what is seen, but on what is unseen. For what is seen is temporary, but what is unseen is eternal."* It is easy to get caught up in the death and miss the resurrection; to see the huge circumstances piling up in our lives and miss the victory that we have already received. If we could stop and think about how many problems we have had in our lives so far…We probably have had millions of problems that we have faced in our lives so far. Many of them were problems that consumed us. But more than likely, we probably don't even remember 90% of all the things that we fretted over in the past. Yet in our lives, we continue to come to the empty tomb and see death. We haven't learned too quickly, we continue to let the problems that come into our lives control us. Our temporary problems steal our eternal victory.

I saw a quote this week that said, "The world offers promises full of emptiness. But Easter offers emptiness full of promise."[34] Let's look at this quote in more depth. The first part says, "The world offers promises full of emptiness."

The world will give you wealth, it will give you relationships, fame and fortune. It promises you a lot—but it will also be taken away. What the world gives you is not lasting! You think that the world and its desires will make you happy, but you will find that it will leave you unsatisfied and keep you searching for the next thing the world can give you. While "Easter offers emptiness full of promise." Empty cross, empty tomb, empty grave-clothes … all are full of promise. We have the promise of the cleansing of sin and the conquering of death. These things will satisfy our souls and they can never be taken away from us.

What Do You Believe About The Resurrection?

The resurrection of Jesus was mostly a hidden event. Jesus didn't rise from the dead to prove to those who had crucified Him that they had made a mistake. Nor did He rise to impress the rulers of His time or to force anyone to believe in Him. Jesus didn't go back to Jerusalem and laugh in their faces or inflict punishment on them. Jesus only showed Himself to those who knew about His love. He made Himself known as the risen Lord only to a handful of His close friends. There is no event in human history that has had such importance, while remaining, at the same time, so unspectacular. No CNN cameras were at the empty tomb covering it for weeks straight. It went pretty much unnoticed by most of the world. Jesus didn't show Himself to the whole world when He rose. He told His followers to let the whole world know. We believe in the resurrection because of the testimony of the disciples—the first people to be skeptical of the resurrection.

How can we believe the disciples? Maybe they made up the story. Do you think that they would be willing to die for a story they made up? No one dies for something that they know is not true. If it was a lie, you would think one of the disciples would have given in under the pressure... but they were all willing to die for what they knew was true. When Jesus was arrested, the disciples ran—they feared they would be taken and killed along with Jesus. They lived in hiding for three days, scared and petrified. Something had to happen to embolden these scaredy cats. What happened? They witnessed the fact that Jesus was alive and they were willing to die to proclaim the truth.

The evidence for Jesus' resurrection is so strong that nobody would question it except for two things: One reason people question the resurrection is that it is a very unusual event. (It is so out of the ordinary and you cannot explain it by logic or science). If you are the kind of person that has to logically figure out everything with your human mind—you will not accept God working in this miraculous way. God can do things our minds and science could never explain. We need to look with eyes of faith knowing that God transcends science and our logic! The second reason people doubt the resurrection is, if you believed it really happened, you would have to change the way you live.[35]

People don't want to change their behavior or lifestyle. You cannot believe Jesus died for your sins and conquered death on your behalf—and then think it doesn't change how you are supposed to live. The resurrection changes everything! The resurrection means we have life.

Jesus says that He is the Light of the World—in Him there is no darkness. Jesus, the light of the world, was put into a tomb, and the tomb was sealed. The tomb is dark; death represents darkness. But we all know that darkness cannot contain light. If you light a match in the dark, you will see that light is more powerful than darkness. In the same way the Light of the World overpowers the darkness of sin and death. HE IS RISEN! And we too will rise if we believe in the death and resurrection of Jesus Christ. The last enemy has been destroyed. The King above all Kings has conquered death.

The women and the disciples had all of the evidence in front of them. They had to make a decision whether or not to believe. Today the choice is yours. Today you are standing at the empty tomb. You must figure out what you believe with the evidence you have in front of you.

The Resurrection Changes Everything

Once the disciples saw the risen Lord, they were never the same. They were willing to do anything and go anywhere. They were willing to do that for the rest of their lives because they were convinced who Jesus was. I know the resurrection happened 2000 years ago—we didn't see it happen, and it has been so long ago that we may be emotionally detached. But just imagine how you would feel if it happened today, if Jesus died on Friday and on Sunday morning He walked into your church service. Your tired yawns from listening to the sermon would turn into weak knees, as you saw the Risen Savior. Your life would be dramatically altered. Don't let time dissolve the impact of this message. Someone once said, "I am going to live like Jesus died yesterday, rose today, and is coming back tomorrow." We need to live with that kind of intensity.

We must see—without death there is no resurrection. You have to die before you can be resurrected. Jesus tells us in Luke 9:23, *"Then he said to them all: If anyone would come after me, he must deny himself and take up his cross daily and follow me."* Pick up your cross daily—that means to die to yourself and your desires each day. If you die to yourself, you can be resurrected with Him. But you cannot expect to be resurrected if you are unwilling to die.

We have a lot to sing and shout about because of the empty tomb.

There was a British minister who began to notice some uneasiness in his throat and a dragging in his leg. When he went to the doctor, he found that he had an incurable disease. His muscles gradually wasted away, his voice would fail, his throat would soon become unable to swallow. Instead of preaching he would write articles and books. When people started to pity him he would say, "I'm only in the kindergarten of suffering." Gradually his legs became useless…his voice went completely. But he could still shakily hold a pen. On Easter morning, just a few weeks before his death, he wrote a letter to his daughter. In it he said, "It is terrible to wake up on Easter morning and have no voice to shout HE IS RISEN! But it would be still more terrible to have a voice and not want to shout.[36]

We all have a voice…I hope we desire to shout "Jesus is risen!"

As you finish this chapter, I hope you will see that the resurrection does change everything! It changes where we can spend eternity…and it changes how the faithful live their lives on this side of the grave. We die to ourselves, so that we can take part in His resurrection.

Releasing the Guilt

Super Sunday is a time when many family and friends gather together. You talk about how you spent this time in the past years. There is food all over the place. There is lots of laughter and joy. Super Sunday...that is what our society calls "Super Bowl Sunday." It is the most watched thing on TV, and it is the most expensive time for businesses to advertise. For a couple of weeks the media has special programming, there is heavy gambling, and hundreds of millions of dollars are made on T-shirts and hats. Our society thinks that this is the biggest Sunday of the year. But as Christians, we know that the first "Super Sunday" took place thousands of years before the Super Bowl came to be. Approximately 30AD, the Son of God rose from the grave—never to die again.[37]

You can't have a Sunday any better than that, even if your favorite team wins the Super Bowl, because the Super Sunday that Jesus rose from the dead has profound meaning for our lives. It means that one day we too will rise from the dead. Easter Sunday is the real Super Sunday celebration.

On the same day that Jesus rose from the dead He visited the disciples in the upper room. He came to bring them the peace that they longed for. We read this story in John 20.

> [19] *On the evening of that first day of the week, when the disciples were together, with the doors locked for fear of the Jews, Jesus came and stood among them and said, "Peace be with you!"*
>
> [20] *After he said this, he showed them his hands and side. The disciples were overjoyed when they saw the Lord.*
>
> [21] *Again Jesus said, "Peace be with you! As the Father has sent me, I am sending you."*
>
> [22] *And with that he breathed on them and said, "Receive the Holy Spirit.*
>
> [23] *If you forgive anyone his sins, they are forgiven; if you do not forgive them, they are not forgiven."*

Jesus Came To Give Peace

Verse 19 says that this occurred on the first day of the week. It was the same day that He rose from the dead. Jesus came and found the disciples cowering in the upper room with the doors locked. The disciples were confused and fearful. They were scared that the people who had killed Jesus would soon be coming after them. A few days earlier, the disciples had left Jesus by Himself because they were scared for their lives. The disciples were full of guilt for having left Jesus.

They were held hostage because of their fears and guilt. They were not locked in prison by the Jews, but they were locked in a room because of their own feelings.

Even though the doors were locked, and there was no way for someone to enter, Jesus appeared in the room. Here they were, locked inside because of fear, doubt, confusion, and guilt, and Jesus broke through all of that and showed Himself to them. You notice that Jesus did not take chain cutters and cut the chain or break the lock that was on the door. That source of the disciples' guilt was still there. But Jesus showed Himself through it. It was up to the disciples to be set free from the guilt that they felt and go unlock the door. Jesus did not unlock the door—He just gave the disciples good reason to go unlock it and go out into freedom again.

Jesus came with an important message for His disciples. The first words that the Risen Lord spoke to them were, *"Peace be with you."* This phrase was a common Hebrew greeting. But Jesus intended for it to be more than just an average greeting. To let them know it was more than just to greet them, He said it a second time, *"Peace be with you."* He said it a third time to Thomas in verse 26. Jesus was trying to make His message clear. The message…I have come back to bring you my peace. The disciples' lives were anything but peaceful. They had external things that caused them to be scared, but worse than the external fear was the internal guilt that they felt. They had no peace inside because they denied Christ.

Some of you may be able to identify with that. It is a horrible feeling not to have peace in your spirit. They just couldn't forgive themselves for leaving Jesus by Himself to die. They were held hostage by their past mistakes. But it all changed when they saw the Risen Lord's hands and His side. Verse 20 says that the disciples were overjoyed. They were carrying around an overwhelming guilt—I have turned from the master…I am scum…I don't deserve to have any peace or to feel good about myself. Maybe that is you. Something you have done in your life has resulted in an inability to feel true peace in your life. You have denied the Lord, just like the disciples. You have locked yourself in your prison of guilt. Even though the Risen Lord has shown Himself to you—you still haven't worked up the courage to go unlock the door. You have not accepted the peace that Jesus has come to give you. If you have caught a glimpse of the Risen Christ, you should be able to see like the disciples did…that the Risen Christ takes away our sin and our guilt. That's what Jesus' resurrection means. He has conquered sin and death. Why do you like to hang on to it?

    Satan loves to have you locked up in your guilt. He doesn't want you to see the Risen Christ. The Apostle Paul talks about the peace we have in the Risen Lord. In Philippians 4:7 he says, *"And the peace of God, which transcends all understanding, will guard your hearts and your minds in Christ Jesus."* Oh how I want to have that kind of peace. The peace in my heart that comes from knowing that God does not condemn me. Today is the day you can have reassurance that God does not want to hold the past over your heads. He wants to set you free from your guilt. Romans 8:1 says, *"Therefore, there is now no condemnation for those who are in Christ*

Jesus." If we are found in Christ we cannot be condemned because when God looks at us He sees His Son...He does not see our sins because the blood of Christ has washed them away.

Sometimes it is hard to let go of the bad things we have done in the past. Put yourself in Peter's shoes. I am sure that he was retracing his steps in his mind the last night of Jesus' life. The crowd came to arrest Jesus, and he ran. Then later that night he was asked three times if he knew Jesus—and all three times he denied Him. How horrible it must have been for Peter to relive those moments in his mind, to remember every detail of how he had failed the Lord. He was in a prison of guilt. I am sure there are some people who are reading this who are in the same situation that Peter and the other disciples found themselves in. You re-think over and over again the times that you have denied Jesus. Jesus knew the disciples denied Him—yet He came back to let them know, "I forgive you." And He has forgiven you too. You need to drop the burden of guilt.

Did you know that when people have a limb amputated, they can still feel pain where that limb was. Say someone got their leg amputated—they can still feel pain in that leg. Even though that leg is not there anymore, their brain still receives an impulse telling them that the leg hurts. The brain will not accept the fact that the leg is gone. It is called "phantom pain." Even though it is not there, it still hurts. Well as Christians we can experience that phantom pain. We have done things in the past that we are not proud of. We have painful memories. We have come to God and asked His forgiveness for those things. And according to 1 John 1:9, God is faithful and has forgiven us. God has forgiven us for the things we have done and amputates the sin from our lives. The sin is not there anymore. But our brains will not let go of our past. We feel the hurt that our past sins have caused. Why do we feel that hurt when God has removed those sins from us? We are experiencing "Phantom sin." Sin that is not there but still causes us pain.[38]

Today we need to realize that the Risen Lord has freed us from the sins we have committed. And we need to stop reliving them.

Jesus didn't leave the disciples in this room feeling guilty. He didn't rise and go to heaven right away. He came to tell them, "I have risen from the dead to overcome sin—I have overcome your sin." He tells us the same thing today. In John 8:36 Jesus says, *"So if the Son sets you free, you will be free indeed."* You are free; why stay locked up in your room of guilt?

Jesus Came Back To Release Us For Ministry

Jesus offered us peace and all we have to do is accept

it. Jesus then wants us to go and do His work. He wants us to go and share this peace with other people who need to hear about the peace found in the Risen Christ. Jesus says in the last part of verse 21, *"As the Father has sent me, I am sending you."* The disciples couldn't complete their ministry in that locked room. They couldn't minister to others because they were paralyzed with guilt. It was absolutely necessary for them to go and unlock the door and receive the peace offered from God. It's the same way with us. We cannot minister if we are locked in our rooms of guilt. Some of you may think, "I cannot minister because of my past. I denied Him by the way I lived so I can't be used for Him." Stop and think about this: Could you imagine what this world would be like today if the disciples said that same thing. "I cannot minister because of my past denials of Jesus." If the disciples would not have accepted Jesus' peace, the church would not be the church today. Nobody would have heard the life changing message of Jesus because of the guilt of the disciples. How devastating it would have been for you and me, if the disciples had remained in that room. And if we remain in our guilt, saying we are not worthy to do things for God, there will be many in this world who will not hear about the peace that they can have in our Risen Savior. Don't deprive people of something that can change their eternity just because you let Satan keep you in a prison from which Jesus came to set you free.

    Jesus wants us to go and do His work. And the great thing is; He has given us the power to do it. Verse 22 says, *"And with that he breathed on them and said, Receive the Holy*

Spirit." He gave the disciples the Holy Spirit to do the work He called them to. The disciples could not change the world with their own skills. Nor can we change the world with our own efforts. Jesus breathed on them and they received the Holy Spirit. The breath of God symbolizes life. In Genesis 1, God formed man out of dust. Man was still dead until God breathed in his nostrils and the man became a living being. The Bible also says in Ezekiel 37 that Ezekiel was surrounded by a valley full of lifeless, dry bones. He prophesized and all the bones came together to make bodies…but they were still dead. Then God breathed into them and they lived. The breath of God symbolizes life. Without God breathing on us and releasing His Holy Spirit in us—our ministries are dead. They are just shells. Jesus desires to give us His peace and the power of His Spirit.

But we have a choice to make today…just like the choice the disciples had to make. We may be bound up with guilt in our lives but today we stand face to face with the Risen Lord. He has come to extend His peace to us. Will you lay down the guilt?

> I received an email with a story about a little boy who went to visit his grandparents on their farm. He was given a slingshot to play with out in the woods. He practiced in the woods, but he could never hit the target. Getting a little discouraged, he headed back for dinner. As he was walking back he saw

his Grandmother's pet duck. Out of impulse, he let the slingshot fly, hit the duck and killed it. He was shocked and grieved. In a panic, he hid the dead duck in the wood pile, only to see his sister watching. Sally had seen it all, but she said nothing. After lunch the next day Grandma said, "Sally, let's wash the dishes." But Sally said, "Grandma, Johnny told me he wanted to help with the dishes." Then she whispered to him, "Remember the duck?" So Johnny did the dishes. Later that day, Grandpa asked if the children wanted to go out fishing. But Grandma says, "No, I need Sally to help make supper." Sally just smiled and said, "Johnny said he wanted to help make supper tonight." She whispered again to Johnny, "Remember the duck?" So Sally went fishing and Johnny stayed at home to make supper. After several days of Johnny doing both his chores and Sally's, he finally couldn't stand it any longer. He went to his Grandma and confessed that he had killed the duck. Grandma knelt beside him and gave him a big hug. "I know you did. I was standing at the window and I saw the whole thing. But because I loved you, I forgave you. I was just wondering how long you would let Sally make a slave of you."

Maybe you are being played like Johnny was. Satan wants to control our lives because he knows the things that we have done. And whenever God wants us to do something for Him, Satan whispers in our ears, "You can't do that; remember the duck?" He keeps you in slavery by your guilt. But today God is reaching for you, saying, "I know the things you have done...I've seen it. But I love you and have already forgiven you. I have risen from the dead, and I have already taken away the guilt of sin. You just need to let go of your guilt."

Living in the past is like trying to walk backwards everywhere you go. It will slow you down and you are bound to be tripped up. Forgiveness moves you forward. Some people believe that their sin is so bad that Jesus can't forgive them. They may believe that they have sinned too much. "Jesus can forgive everyone else's sin, but He can't forgive mine." The gospel of Jesus that can save everybody else, the blood of Jesus that can cleanse everyone else...can cleanse and save you too. Know today that Jesus' blood can cover your sin!

ROAD TO EMMAUS

Karl Barth, the famous theologian and preacher, was on a streetcar one day in Basel, Switzerland, where he lectured. A tourist to the city climbed on and sat down next to Barth. The two men started chatting with each other. "Are you new to the city?" Barth inquired. "Yes," said the tourist. "Is there anything you would particularly like to see in this city?" asked Barth. "Yes," he said, "I'd love to meet the famous theologian Karl Barth. Do you know him?" Barth replied, "Well as a matter of fact, I do. I give him a shave every morning." The tourist got off the streetcar quite delighted. He went back to his hotel saying to himself, "Wow—I met Karl Barth's barber today." He talked with Karl Barth and he didn't even realize it.[39]

Jesus did not rise from the dead and sneak off to heaven without showing Himself. Many people saw the Risen Lord. In this chapter you will see two disciples who were walking along the road with Jesus, but just like the man in Switzerland, these disciples did not recognize who they were talking too. Luke 24 says:

[13] Now that same day two of them were going to a village called Emmaus, about seven miles

from Jerusalem. [14] *They were talking with each other about everything that had happened.* [15] *As they talked and discussed these things with each other, Jesus himself came up and walked along with them;* [16] *but they were kept from recognizing him.*

[17] *He asked them, "What are you discussing together as you walk along?"*

They stood still, their faces downcast. [18] *One of them, named Cleopas, asked him, "Are you only a visitor to Jerusalem and do not know the things that have happened there in these days?"*

[19] *"What things?" he asked.*

"About Jesus of Nazareth," they replied. "He was a prophet, powerful in word and deed before God and all the people. [20] *The chief priests and our rulers handed him over to be sentenced to death, and they crucified him;* [21] *but we had hoped that he was the one who was going to redeem Israel. And what is more, it is the third day since all this took place.* [22] *In addition, some of our women amazed us. They went to the tomb early this morning* [23] *but didn't find his body. They came and told us that they had seen a vision of angels, who said he was alive.* [24] *Then some of our companions went to the tomb and found it just as the women had said, but him they did not see."*

[25] He said to them, "How foolish you are, and how slow of heart to believe all that the prophets have spoken! [26] Did not the Christ have to suffer these things and then enter his glory?" [27] And beginning with Moses and all the Prophets, he explained to them what was said in all the Scriptures concerning himself.

[28] As they approached the village to which they were going, Jesus acted as if he were going farther. [29] But they urged him strongly, "Stay with us, for it is nearly evening; the day is almost over." So he went in to stay with them.

[30] When he was at the table with them, he took bread, gave thanks, broke it and began to give it to them. [31] Then their eyes were opened and they recognized him, and he disappeared from their sight. [32] They asked each other, "Were not our hearts burning within us while he talked with us on the road and opened the Scriptures to us?"

[33] They got up and returned at once to Jerusalem. There they found the Eleven and those with them, assembled together [34] and saying, "It is true! The Lord has risen and has appeared to Simon." [35] Then the two told what had happened on the way, and how Jesus was recognized by them when he broke the bread.

Have You Lost Your Hope In Jesus?

This story is taking place on the same day that Jesus rose from the dead. The first 12 verses of this chapter talked about how Jesus' tomb was empty...and then in verse 13, it says, *"Now that same day."* On Easter day, two men were walking seven miles from Jerusalem to a town called Emmaus. A lot of things had taken place the prior two days in Jerusalem. Just a couple of days before, on Friday, Jesus had died on the cross. Then Sunday morning came and there was quite a commotion going on. There was speculation that Jesus had actually risen from the dead. The woman saw that the tomb was empty and they claimed that they saw an angel telling them that Jesus was alive. A couple of the disciples also went to the tomb and saw that it was empty. These two men who were traveling to Emmaus knew about everything that had happened that morning.

When Jesus approached these two men, it is no surprise that He found them talking about the weekend's events. It's natural to want to talk about something incredible that has just happened. Some people leave a ballgame or a concert and can't help talking about it for the next few days. When I was a senior in high school, we had a great basketball team. What an exciting time in my life. We played the number 1 ranked team in the state during our regional game...and we beat them! I remember the joy that we had that night as we talked about different plays in the game. Then we kept winning and we made it all the way to state. This had never happened at my high school before—but it was happening to us. We couldn't help but to think how great it would be to win a game down at state. We started the state game by going ahead 15-0. It looked like our hopes were coming true. It was coming true! But all of a sudden, out of nowhere, the team we were playing came back and beat us. We were shocked. We went from being elated one moment, to being discouraged really quickly.

We had many conversations the next several weeks about that game. We couldn't get our minds off of it. It seemed like every conversation we had came back to that game. Sharing about how we thought we had it...and reliving the disappointment. These disciples were experiencing something far greater. They witnessed the cross...and now the talk of an empty tomb. I would imagine that every conversation they had came back to Jesus being dead. They couldn't help but talk about it because it was the most significant thing that had ever happened in their lives.

As they were walking and talking, Jesus came up and asked them, "What are you talking about?" The disciples couldn't believe that this stranger had no idea what they were talking about. How could He not have heard about what had taken place? One of them said to Jesus, *"Are you only a visitor to Jerusalem and do not know the things that have happened there in these days?"* There were many visitors in Jerusalem during this time of year. This time each year Jerusalem would double in size because everyone wanted to be in the Holy City as they celebrated the huge Passover festival. So these men thought, "He must be a visitor." But even visitors would know what happened to Jesus. News like this spread very quickly. A public execution would be the hot topic to talk about—especially when it was someone who was so popular. Jesus was known throughout the land. Jesus was tried publicly, and there was a tremendous ordeal that day in Jerusalem. A large crowed gathered and made a huge uproar. They screamed, "Crucify him! Crucify him!" There was no way you could be in Jerusalem and not know about this event! So these disciples were shocked that this stranger didn't know what had happened to Jesus. Of course Jesus knew what happened because it happened to Him, but He played along. Jesus asked the disciples, *"What things* (are you talking about)*?"*

The two men talked about the death of Jesus, and the questionable resurrection. As the two men talked you could tell that they were not believers in the resurrection. The women said that Jesus had risen that morning, yet these two men didn't wait around to find out if what the women said was true. They either had some very urgent business that couldn't wait or they doubted that this story was true. I know that I wouldn't have left so quickly if I believed something like that could be true. Imagine that you are out of town because a loved one died—someone you placed a lot of hope in. Then you hear people say that this person may be alive after all. You hear the news that there is a possibility that they may be alive…yet you decide to pack up and drive home that day anyway. I know that if there was any possibility that this was true, I would have waited around to see. But these two men didn't wait.

Look at the demeanor of these two men. Verse 17 says that they stood still, their faces downcast. There was no joy in their faces thinking that Jesus had risen. Their faces told the story. But from their mouths they said in verse 21, *"but we had hoped that he was the one who was going to redeem Israel."* Do you hear the past tense? We <u>had hoped</u> that He was the one. We had hope that He was the Messiah that was going to redeem us. We thought He would free us from the oppression of the Roman government. But obviously He wasn't the one. The end of verse 19 tells what they thought of Him, *"He was a prophet, powerful in word and deed before God and all the people."* Looking back after His death, they were not so optimistic. They had respect for Jesus as a man of God, as a prophet—a good teacher of the things of God, but they did not see Him as the Messiah anymore. Before His death they held out high hopes for Him that He was the Messiah. They followed Jesus for three years. They saw all of the amazing things that He did. They had placed all of their hopes in Him. But when Jesus died, their hopes died with Him. He is not the One we thought.

Maybe you have lost hope in Jesus. Maybe, like these two men, something dramatic has happened in your life and Jesus doesn't seem to be who you thought He was. You feel like you can no longer put your trust or hopes in Him. Maybe because of the things that have happened you no longer believe that He is the Messiah, the one who will save you. Let's look at Jesus' answer to those who lose their hope in Him.

Has God Revealed Any Truth To You?

As Jesus listened to the men traveling to Emmaus, He had enough and said to them in verses 25-26, *"How foolish you are, and how slow of heart to believe all that the prophets have spoken! Did not the Christ have to suffer these things and then enter his glory?"* Jesus rebukes them. "Why is it so hard for you to believe? It is all right there in front of you. Read the scriptures." These disciples were so caught up in the last three days, that they missed God's larger plan. Jesus said, "Yes, everything that you are saying took place, but you are missing how it fits in with all of the scriptures." Jesus gave these two men a Bible lesson that day. What a treat for these two disciples. They got to walk with Jesus all day long and listen to Jesus interpret the Old Testament. In verse 27 it says, *"And beginning with Moses and all the Prophets, he explained to them what was said in all the Scriptures concerning himself."* Jesus spoke to them about Moses and all the prophets. This tells us that Jesus didn't just pick out one verse in the Old Testament that could be an interpretation of His rising from the dead. Jesus used the entire Old Testament to show them that this was God's plan all along. Jesus began with Moses, with the law…and how the law pointed to His coming. Jesus may have said something like the Apostle Paul did in Galatians 3:24. *"So the law was put in charge to lead us to Christ."* The law points us to Christ.

Then He shared about how the prophets spoke of the coming of the Messiah. He could have spoken about Zechariah, saying that the king will come riding in on a donkey, like Jesus did at the triumphal entry. Micah says that He will come from Bethlehem; Jesus was born in Bethlehem. Isaiah talks about how He will be born of a virgin…and how He will be pierced and crushed for our sins. The book of Psalms tell us how the soldiers were going to divide His clothing and that none of his bones would be broken. I would have loved to have heard Jesus speak to them about the many examples in the Old Testament that pointed to Him.

Could you imagine Jesus spending the day with you and interpreting the scriptures for you? In Verse 32 the two men say, *"Were not our hearts burning within us while he talked with us on the road and opened the Scriptures to us?"* The Word was made alive to them. "Burned within them." These two guys were people who read the Bible, but they had never heard it like that before. Their eyes were opened to the scriptures.

Unfortunately, many people today sit down and read the Bible like any other book. No emotion, no passion. Nothing they read stirs their spirits. Some people get more excited reading a romance novel or a mystery thriller than they do the Living Word of God. Jesus opened up the word to these two men. Jesus brought the understanding that they needed…to see the truth. I have said many times that people can read the Living Word of God and get nothing out of it. They are blinded to the meaning to it. They are just reading words on a page. We need to have the Holy Spirit working in our lives to bring the understanding to us. If the Holy Spirit is working in us as we read the Bible, our hearts will burn within us. The Bible will come alive. We will notice things that we have never seen before. God will reveal new things about himself. In Psalm 119:97 the Psalmist says, *"Oh, how I love your law! I meditate on it all day long."* And in Psalm 119:103, *"How sweet are your words to my taste, sweeter than honey to my mouth!"* Do you think that the Psalmist's heart burned within him as he read and meditated on God's Word? I hope God is revealing new truth to you as you read and meditate on His Word.

Maybe you have lost your hope in Jesus because you haven't been getting any new truths about Him. It is easy to become content in our faith. Before His death—the men were content in what they knew of Jesus. They had seen His miracles and heard His teachings, but after His death that wasn't enough. They needed more of Jesus to be revealed to them. Yesterday's hopes were gone…they needed to know more about Jesus today. As Christians, it is not acceptable for us to be in the same place in our walk as we were five year ago. Five years from now we should be light years ahead of where we are now. We need to be filled with the Spirit and the Word each day. We need God to reveal more of Himself to us…or we too may lose the hope that we had in Him yesterday.

This passage says that once they reached their destination, Jesus was going to keep on going. The disciples did not want that. They wanted more time with this man because He stirred their spirits. Their time with Jesus completely changed the outlook of their lives. They went from desperation to regaining their hope again. That is what happens when we spend time with God, and when we let Him speak in our lives. He is able to put a passion in our hearts. We will want more time with Him!

I believe there is a good lesson in these verses for us today. A person can see the Risen Lord and not even recognize Him. These men walked with Jesus all day long—yet they did not know it was Jesus. We too could have Jesus in our lives and yet not see Him for who He really is. We need our eyes to be opened, we need to catch a glimpse of who He really is.

Humble King To Conquering King

THOMAS' UNBELIEF

As humans we are prone to ask the question, "Why?" We are prone to question…to doubt…to want answers…to want proof. We get it at an early age. Actually we were born that way. Before a child can speak you can look into his eyes and you can see him taking everything in—he wants to know more. And then when the child begins to speak, watch out. You hear the famous question—"Why?" I have had a couple of opportunities to be in a car with young kids. For hours and hours they will ask you, "Why?" You give them the answer, and they say again, "Why?" Then you say some more and they say again, "Why?" Finally you have enough and you just say "because". These kids want to know more. They question everything. But questions and doubts continue with us through our whole lives. We want to know more than we know now. It is easier to doubt the things that we cannot prove, than it is to accept them.[40] Let's take a look at John 20.

> [24] Now Thomas (called Didymus), one of the Twelve, was not with the disciples when Jesus came.
> [25] So the other disciples told him, "We have seen the Lord!"

> But he said to them, "Unless I see the nail marks in his hands and put my finger where the nails were, and put my hand into his side, I will not believe it."
>
> [26] A week later his disciples were in the house again, and Thomas was with them. Though the doors were locked, Jesus came and stood among them and said, "Peace be with you!"
>
> [27] Then he said to Thomas, "Put your finger here; see my hands. Reach out your hand and put it into my side. Stop doubting and believe."
>
> [28] Thomas said to him, "My Lord and my God!"
>
> [29] Then Jesus told him, "Because you have seen me, you have believed; blessed are those who have not seen and yet have believed."
>
> [30] Jesus did many other miraculous signs in the presence of his disciples, which are not recorded in this book. [31] But these are written that you may believe that Jesus is the Christ, the Son of God, and that by believing you may have life in his name.

Sometimes We Doubt

I want to share a quote that shows the doubt we tend to have. "If you tell a man that there are 581,678, 934,341 stars in the universe, he'll believe you. But if a sign says, "Fresh Paint," he has to make a personal investigation."[41] He has to find out for himself. He is not going to believe a sign or what someone else says. Today we are going to look at Thomas. He questioned, he doubted, and he wanted to touch in order to believe.

The passage right before this one shows us that Jesus came back and showed Himself to His disciples. They saw the Risen Lord, but it says that Thomas was not with them when the Lord came back. A week had gone by since Jesus had appeared to the disciples. They had no clue if Jesus would ever show Himself again. Jesus didn't leave them a schedule of His next appearances. Jesus didn't look at His daily planner and say, "I am scheduled to be back in a week. Look for me a week from today." No, they had no idea if they would see Him again.

The disciples told Thomas about Jesus being alive, but Thomas doubted that what the disciples said was true. And that is what we remember Thomas for. If I asked you about Thomas, my guess is that the first thing to pop in most people's mind would be that he doubted that Jesus rose from the dead. This is why he is called "Doubting Thomas". We think of Thomas in a negative sense. But there is another side to Thomas as well. Thomas means Twin. This is not to say that Thomas has a split personality, but it does show that Thomas is known for two different behaviors. We already know that he is known as a doubter, but something that is less known about Thomas is that he was loyal and willing to die to follow Jesus. Back in John 11, Jesus was going to go back to Judea. The disciples all knew that people in that area wanted Him dead, so they tried to talk Jesus out of going back. But

Jesus was determined to go. So Thomas said to the rest of the disciples in John 11:16, *"Let us also go, that we may die with him."* Thomas was willing to die for Jesus. He was loyal to his master. Why don't we remember Thomas that way? Why isn't he called "Courageous Thomas"?

Why does Thomas get the bad rap among the disciples? All of the disciples had trouble living out a perfect life of faith. Look at Peter. He was the spokesman of the early church, yet we see that he denied knowing Jesus three times. All of the disciples ran away from Jesus when He was arrested. Isn't it interesting to see that even the people who followed Jesus every day for three years and saw all of the amazing miracles had troubles with doubts.

As we look at Thomas' life, it's easy to see that we can be a lot like him. At one point in our life, we can stand up tall and say, "I will go wherever you want me to go…I will die for you", and at another point we find ourselves struggling with doubts about our faith. The main question for Thomas in this passage was, Who is Jesus? Thomas doubted that Jesus was who He claimed to be. If Thomas believed that Jesus was the Messiah sent from God, then he would have had no problem believing that Jesus had risen from the dead.

Thomas was having a crisis of faith. He witnessed Jesus' death. "That wasn't supposed to happen. How can I make sense of this?" Thomas came to the point where he said, "Unless He shows Himself to me I can't believe that He is alive and that He is the Messiah." I need proof! In the movie "Simon Birch", Simon says to a friend, "You need to have faith." The friend replies, "I do have faith, I just want evidence to back it up." The friend wanted evidence to back up his faith. God has called us to a life of faith. He has never said that we are going to understand everything in this life. Faith is trusting in God even though it doesn't make sense.

Can you see yourself in Thomas? Times get tough and it shakes your faith. Doubts are usually brought on by a traumatic experience. We suffer a big blow...and it leaves us doubting who God is. We usually don't doubt God when things are going well. When we get a promotion at work, the family is healthy, the money keeps coming in, our friends are around...we have total confidence in God. But when we are facing family problems, troubled relationships, financial difficulties, or unhealthy family members...we may see God a little differently. That is what Thomas was dealing with here. Throughout Jesus' life, Thomas was gladly by His side. Thomas would boldly confess that Jesus is the Christ, and that He came from God. Why not? Things were good—Jesus was performing miracles, and His teachings made a lot of sense..."Yep I believe He is who He says He is." But Thomas received a blow to his faith when Jesus was killed, and the doubts entered his mind. This life will always throw things at us which will give us reasons to doubt. But we need to know the unchangeable truth that Jesus is always God and He is always in control. Hebrews 13:8 says, *"Jesus Christ is the same yesterday and today and forever."* He never changes. When things are going well He is the same as when things are going poorly. It is our insecurities that bring doubts. God has not changed, just our perception of God has changed.

Encountering The Risen Christ Removes All Doubts

We all go through seasons of doubt where things don't make sense, where God doesn't make sense to us. Maybe you think you are the only one who has doubts. We beat ourselves up because of some doubts that we have. But as Thomas worked through his doubts, he had more confidence in his faith than he ever had before! He now knew that not even death can stop Jesus. After a week of doubting, Thomas dropped to the ground and said, "My Lord and my God." Basically, "I should have never doubted you. You are most certainly God." His trust in God had been renewed and we see that he was now ready to die because his faith was so strong. Earlier he had said that he was ready to die, but when Jesus was arrested Thomas ran away to save his own life. Then, after seeing Jesus conquer death, Thomas did die for his faith. History shows that Thomas followed the Great Commission and went to India where he was thrown into a fiery furnace and pierced by spears. Thomas paid the ultimate price to follow Christ. Yet we label him as "Doubting Thomas".

Jesus says to Thomas in verse 29, *"Because you have seen me, you have believed; blessed are those who have not seen and yet have believed."* We are to believe by faith, not by sight. We don't have the same benefit as Thomas. We will not physically see Him with our eyes, yet Jesus wants us to make the same decision that Thomas made, "My Lord and my God." Jesus was saying this because He knew many, many generations of the church would not see Him, yet they would believe anyway. I have heard many people say, "Why doesn't God just show Himself in a mighty way like He did in the Bible, then I will believe." Where is the faith in that? We live in a very visual society where people need to see in order to believe.

When the missionary children were called in for dinner, their mother said, "Be sure to wash your hands." The little boy scowled and said, "Germs and Jesus. Germs and Jesus. That's all I hear, and I've never seen either one of them."[42] There are many things that we don't see and yet we believe in them. You can't see air, but you know it is there or you wouldn't be alive. You can't see gravity, but walk off of a tall building and I'll bet you would start believing in it pretty quickly. We can be sure something exists even though we can't see it. We can believe in Jesus without seeing because His life was written down for us. John says in verse 31, *"These are written that you may believe Jesus is the Christ."* John knew you wouldn't see all of the things that he saw, but you can read them and know that these stories are true. John says that there is so much more that Jesus did that is not written down. I wish there would have been more written about Jesus' life. I wish I could read about other miracles that He performed, other teachings that He taught. Wouldn't it be great to have a library full of books that described the different things that Jesus did? The last verse in the book of John says, *"Jesus did many other things as well. If everyone of them were written down, I suppose that even the whole world would not have room for the books that would be written."* Jesus did so much more than what we have read about in the Bible. But we have all that we need in the Bible to help us understand what Jesus did for us, and to know without a shadow of a doubt that He is God and that He conquered death on our behalf.

Jesus leaves us with a challenge: *"Stop doubting and believe."* I realize that many of the people reading this might be the faithful. But as we looked at this chapter, the disciples were the faithful—following Jesus for three years, night and day. Yet the faithful desperately needed an encounter with the risen Christ. If we encounter the risen Christ today, I guarantee it will change the way we are living. It will change us, just as it changed Thomas and the rest of the disciples.

Reminded Of The Gospel

There is a story of a boy named Philip—he was 9 years old and he joined a Sunday school class for 8 year olds. The class did not welcome Philip to their group. It was not because he was older—it was because he was different. He suffered from Down's Syndrome and the kids would laugh at him because of his appearance and slow responses. One Sunday around Easter time the Sunday school teacher gathered some plastic eggs that pull apart in the middle. She passed one out to everyone in her Sunday school class, including Philip. She told the children to bring the egg back next week with a symbol inside that represents "new life." During the week, the kids were looking for things to put in their egg that represented new life. The next Sunday came and the teacher gathered the eggs and started to open them up. She opened the first egg and there was a beautiful flower. The children "oohed" and "aahed" at the lovely symbol of new life. The teacher opened up another egg and inside was a butterfly. A butterfly was another great example of new life. The teacher picked up a few others and showed the class what was in them. Finally she picked up the last one and opened it. There was nothing in it. The class started to yell that it is unfair that this person didn't do their assignment. But Philip, the outcast, tugged on the teacher's shirt and said, "this one is mine, and I did do it." The teacher said, "It is empty. What do you mean you did it?" Philip replied, "It's empty because I have new life because the tomb is empty."[43]

New life for us does not come because a flower blooms or because a bud blossoms on a tree. New life comes to us through the empty tomb. Thanks to Philip in this story for reminding us that new life is all about the empty tomb. In 1 Corinthians 15, Paul shares why we can believe that the resurrection really took place.

> [1] Now, brothers, I want to remind you of the gospel I preached to you, which you received and on which you have taken your stand. [2] By this gospel you are saved, if you hold firmly to the word I preached to you. Otherwise, you have believed in vain.
>
> [3] For what I received I passed on to you as of first importance: that Christ died for our sins according to the Scriptures, [4] that he was buried, that he was raised on the third day according to the Scriptures, [5] and that he appeared to Peter, and then to the Twelve. [6] After that, he appeared to more than five hundred of the brothers at the same time, most of whom are still living, though some have

fallen asleep. *⁷ Then he appeared to James, then to all the apostles,*

⁸ and last of all he appeared to me also, as to one abnormally born.

⁹ For I am the least of the apostles and do not even deserve to be called an apostle, because I persecuted the church of God. *¹⁰ But by the grace of God I am what I am, and his grace to me was not without effect. No, I worked harder than all of them—yet not I, but the grace of God that was with me.* *¹¹ Whether, then, it was I or they, this is what we preach, and this is what you believed.*

Paul Reminds Them Of The Gospel

Verse 1 starts out, *"Now brothers, I want to remind you of the gospel."* Paul saw something that the Corinthian church needed to be reminded of. They had once received the gospel…they had once lived out the gospel…but now they were somewhat wavering in their faith in the resurrection. They were questioning whether the resurrection really took place. Paul spent this whole chapter talking about the resurrection. Paul received a letter from the Corinthian church…we don't know exactly what the letter to Paul said, or what their questions were…but they had questions about the resurrection of Jesus. In verse 12, Paul says, *"How can some of you say that there is no resurrection of the dead?"* Maybe this is a question in people's minds today. "Did Jesus really rise? Is it that important that I believe Jesus rose from the dead?" Paul says this is a foundational truth. You must believe this. The resurrection is the heart of our faith. You have to believe in the resurrection or your belief in Jesus is in vain. Our hope in Jesus is wrapped up in His coming back to life. We have no hope for the future if Jesus is still in the grave. Believing in the resurrection is not an option for us. It is a must.

Paul reminds them of the <u>absolute</u> fundamentals of the faith in verses 3-4. *"For what I received I passed on to you as of first importance: that Christ died for our sins according to the Scriptures, ⁴ that he was buried, that he was raised on the third day according to the Scriptures,"* Paul confesses that he is not the originator of the gospel. He heard it from others. He was persecuting the church long after Jesus rose from the dead, so he never saw Jesus' resurrected body. He only saw a bright light from heaven and heard His voice. But he said, "What I have received from others I pass on to you as the first importance." First importance. Paul says that there is nothing more important that I have ever said to you or will ever say to you again. "Hear this because it is the most important thing you will ever hear in your life. Jesus died, He was buried, and He was raised from the dead on the third day. If you fail to understand one of these concepts—you fail to understand the gospel message."

This happened just as Scripture said it would. Paul was not passing on a story that was made up by a few of his buddies. He was passing on the fulfillment of prophecies. The Old Testament clearly tells us that the Messiah is going to suffer and die, and then will be raised from the dead. Isaiah 53:11 says, *"After the suffering of his soul, he will see the light of life and be satisfied."* Jesus' death and resurrection is not a clever story, but was predicted hundreds of years in advance. For one reason or another, the Corinthian church was finding it difficult to hold on to this truth. I am sure that in their culture they had a lot of people trying to convince them that the resurrection didn't happen. "The resurrection is nonsense. How can you believe in a wild story like that? Have you ever heard of someone rising from the dead?" There were a couple of theories going around back then. Some believed that His body had been stolen, that He hadn't risen. Some believed that the disciples had taken His body and fooled people into believing that He had risen from the dead. The Pharisee's started that story because they didn't want people to know the truth and follow Jesus. There were others who actually believed that Jesus really didn't die—He was just "mostly dead". They believed that He was just unconscious and He was put in the tomb, and after a few days His body had healed enough that He could get up on His own. We know that this could not be true because the Romans were one of the cruelest nations in the world. They would have made sure that all of the people on the cross were dead before they took them down. The Romans pierced Jesus' side with a spear to make sure that He was dead. The Bible says that water & blood flowed from His side. Medically speaking, this is the sac that surrounds the heart and even the heart itself. After all that Jesus had gone through, there was no way that He was still alive at that point.

Jesus was dead and He was raised again. Paul was writing the Corinth church to be reminded of that. I believe that there are times in our lives when we need to be reminded of the gospel. We have a lot of bad things happening in our lives that come and totally blind us to the truth that we have in God. Much like the Corinthians, we need to be reminded of the gospel. Don't give up hope! Verse 2 says, *"By this gospel you are saved, if you hold firmly to the word I preached to you. Otherwise, you have believed in vain."* We need to hold firmly to the gospel that saves us. The world lives like Jesus stayed in the grave, and, unfortunately, so do many church people. We need to live our lives like we truly believe that He has risen. We are saved if we <u>hold firmly</u> to the gospel. Otherwise we believe in vain. Believing is not enough. We must live out what we believe.

The Gospel Has Many Witnesses

Verses 5-8 say, *"and that he appeared to Peter, and then to the Twelve. After that, he appeared to more than five hundred of the brothers at the same time, most of whom are still living, though some have fallen asleep. Then he appeared to James, then to all the apostles, and last of all he appeared to me also, as to one abnormally born."* We just saw that Paul said one reason you can believe in the resurrection is that scripture tells us it will happen (OT said it before it happened). But if you can't believe that, Paul gives us a second reason to believe that it happened. There were many witnesses who saw Jesus after He rose from the dead. According to the law in the Old Testament, you need to have two or three witnesses to validate your case. As you can see, there were more than two or three witnesses to Jesus' resurrection. There were over five hundred people that could verify that Jesus is alive. Jesus didn't just appear to one person and require that everyone else hear it through the grape vine. If that happened, the one person could have made up the entire thing. But there were many eye witnesses.

The question becomes, can we take these people at their word? This could be one big conspiracy. Maybe the Pharisees are right and they were just making up this story to cause trouble. Maybe the disciples stole His body to make it look like He rose from the dead. If the disciples did steal the body, they were not just facing unpopularity, but beatings, stonings, and executions. They were cut in half, burned at the stake, and crucified upside down for their belief in the resurrection. Every single one of the disciples insisted to their dying breaths that they had physically seen Jesus' body raised from the dead. Don't you think that one of those apostles would have cracked before being beheaded or stoned? If they made up this resurrection thing, don't you think that one of these disciples would have said, "this hoax, or practical joke, is not worth dying for." Not one of the disciples made a deal with the authorities. Men will give their lives for something they believe to be true; they will not give their lives for something they know to be false. I would never die for a practical joke or a hoax. But I would give my life for something I believe in strongly. And that is what the disciples did. The disciples had nothing to gain by dying for a lie that they made up.

For many centuries, men and women in Europe looked out upon the western sea, known as the Atlantic Ocean, and they saw the sun fall into the ocean and disappear. They wondered if there was anything beyond. Most scholars said that you could sail off the edge of the world; that there was nothing out there at all. In fact, Spain's motto was, "There is nothing beyond." One day, Christopher Columbus went on the shiny waters. He sailed off into the sunset as people waited expectantly. Finally, after a long time, the sails reappeared and the crowds gathered. They shouted with joy, and Columbus announced that there was a land beyond the sea that was rich beyond their dreams. It was a glorious paradise. Well for centuries many people have stood beside the dark hole that we call a grave and watched the remains of their loved ones lowered into the earth, and they wondered: is there anything beyond the dark waters of death? Then one day, a young explorer went into the blackness of the pit of death. He sailed off into the unknown. People waited expectantly. Finally, on resurrection morning, as the sun rose in the east, the Son of God stepped forth from the grave and declared, "There is something beyond. There is a paradise beyond your greatest expectations."[44]

There is something beyond death. Death is not the end. When Jesus was hanging on the cross there was a criminal next to Him. This criminal asked Jesus, "Remember me when you come into your kingdom." Jesus said back to the man, "Today you will be with me in paradise." We too have a paradise waiting for us if we see Jesus as King. Not even death can stop the King that we serve. Later in chapter 15 of Corinthians, Paul says, "The last enemy to be destroyed is death." We celebrate because the tomb is empty and death has been defeated. We have hope because our Savior lives and He has made it possible for us to live with Him for eternity.

SERVE THE KING

Even when we are committed to God, there will be times when we fall short of the good intentions that we have in following Him. What happens when we fail? Does that mean that we can't be of any use to God anymore? After the disciples denied Jesus, was there any hope for them? We get our answer here in John 21.

> [15] *When they had finished eating, Jesus said to Simon Peter, "Simon son of John, do you truly love me more than these?"*
>
> *"Yes, Lord," he said, "you know that I love you."*
>
> *Jesus said, "Feed my lambs."*
>
> [16] *Again Jesus said, "Simon son of John, do you truly love me?"*
>
> *He answered, "Yes, Lord, you know that I love you."*
>
> *Jesus said, "Take care of my sheep."*
>
> [17] *The third time he said to him, "Simon son of John, do you love me?"*
>
> *Peter was hurt because Jesus asked him the third time, "Do you love me?" He said,*

"Lord, you know all things; you know that I love you."

Jesus said, "Feed my sheep. [18] I tell you the truth, when you were younger you dressed yourself and went where you wanted; but when you are old you will stretch out your hands, and someone else will dress you and lead you where you do not want to go." [19] Jesus said this to indicate the kind of death by which Peter would glorify God. Then he said to him, "Follow me!"

[20] Peter turned and saw that the disciple whom Jesus loved was following them. (This was the one who had leaned back against Jesus at the supper and had said, "Lord, who is going to betray you?") [21] When Peter saw him, he asked, "Lord, what about him?"

[22] Jesus answered, "If I want him to remain alive until I return, what is that to you? You must follow me." [23] Because of this, the rumor spread among the brothers that this disciple would not die. But Jesus did not say that he would not die; he only said, "If I want him to remain alive until I return, what is that to you?"

[24] This is the disciple who testifies to these things and who wrote them down. We know that his testimony is true.

[25] Jesus did many other things as well. If every

one of them were written down, I suppose that even the whole world would not have room for the books that would be written.

Peter Is Reinstated

Being a follower doesn't mean that we won't mess up once in a while. None of us are going to be perfect followers. We all know the story of Peter. He was a loyal follower of Jesus. He followed Jesus wherever He went for three years. And when Jesus asked the question to the disciples "Who do you say that I am?" It was Peter who boldly said, "You are the Christ, the son of the living God." When Jesus was being arrested, it was Peter who pulled out a small sword and cut off someone's ear. He was going to fight to the death to prevent Jesus' arrest. But it was also Peter that was asked three times whether he was one of Jesus' followers, and all three times he denied even knowing Jesus. Peter's entire life was focused on Jesus, and after he denied Him three times, he wept bitterly. Peter obviously carried around a lot of guilt for denying Jesus.

Before he followed Jesus, he was a fisherman named Simon. It was when he confessed "Jesus is the Christ", that Jesus renamed him Peter. Matthew 16:17-18, *"Blessed are you, Simon son of Jonah, for this was not revealed to you by man, but by my Father in heaven. And I tell you that you are Peter, and on this rock I will build my church, and the gates of Hades will not overcome it."* Peter means rock. Jesus called him a rock. Throughout the rest of Jesus' ministry, Simon was called Peter. For a couple of years Peter could hold his head up high and say "Jesus called me the rock." But after denying Jesus three times, Peter certainly didn't feel like a rock. Notice how Jesus refers to him in this passage. Three times Jesus asks him, "<u>Simon</u> son of John, do you truly love me more than these?" He calls him Simon three times. It must have been hurtful for Peter to hear Jesus call him by his old name. Peter answered, "Lord you know that I love you." Surely every Christian can find themselves making this same statement to God at some point. "Lord you know that I love you even though I did not demonstrate it earlier this week by what I did. Lord you know my heart, you and you alone can discern my true loyalties and my deepest longings. You know that I love you despite my failures." Peter knew that Jesus knew his heart, and could truly see that he loved Him despite the poor choices that he had made.

The very beginning of John 21:15 says, *"When they had finished eating, Jesus said to Simon Peter..."* This occurs after Jesus and the disciples were done eating together, and many scholars believe that Jesus asked him these questions in front of the other disciples. This was most likely meant to be a public restoration of Peter to a position of leadership and trust. All of the disciples knew that Peter had denied Jesus three times. They all knew that spiritually, Peter fell flat on his face. This likely discredited Peter as a leader. I believe that Jesus made this statement in public to allow others to see the restoration that was taking place. "Even though Peter really messed up...I am restoring him and you can have confidence in him and follow him again." Restoration is difficult, and probably very embarrassing for Peter. But without it could he have been given the leadership for the group? He denied Jesus in public, confessing clearly to those in the crowd, "I don't know Jesus." I believe Jesus publicly gives Peter a second chance. And I don't believe it was just a coincidence that Jesus asks Peter three times whether he loved Him. I believe it was purposeful for Peter to be healed from the three times that he had denied Him. Jesus wasn't doing this to Peter in front of everyone to hurt him, but to restore him and his place as a leader in the church.

Peter's Denial Didn't Do Away With His Calling

There is no doubt that Peter is angry and frustrated at himself for denying Jesus. As if he didn't feel bad enough, then Jesus went over and asked him three times if he loved Him. Jesus didn't want to sweep Peter's denials under the rug as if they hadn't happened. He wanted to deal with them first. He wanted Peter to get healing from them, not hide them deep down inside. Peter was hurt that Jesus asked him three times if he loved Him. But after he was restored…I have a mental picture of Jesus lovingly putting His hand on Peter's shoulder with a little smile, "Come, Follow me."

In the end of John 21.19, the last two words Jesus says are, "Follow me." Peter didn't lose his calling. Those were the same words that Peter had heard three years earlier as he was in his fishing boat. "Come, follow me." Peter did not lose his privileges because of his past denials, even though they were very blunt denials. Jesus is all about restoration.

Jesus could have gone to Peter and made him feel horrible that he had denied Him three times. He could have poured salt on Peter's emotional wounds. "Peter, how could you, after all we have been through together? You stood in front of me and told me that you would never deny me. How can I ever believe you again? I thought that you were stronger than that Peter." No, Jesus didn't say any of that. He came to Peter and said, "I want to restore you. I want to use you. Peter, deal with this guilt and move on to what is ahead of you. I have some great things in store for you, if you would just stop living in the past."

Our past does not dictate our future service to Him. In fact He tells Peter three times to "feed my sheep". "Peter, be the shepherd over my flock. I want you to feed the people all the things that you know about me. Lead them Peter." And we know that Jesus used Peter mightily to establish the early church. Could you imagine how the church would be different today if Peter hadn't been given a second chance? Don't give up on the Peters of today.

We have to see that Jesus is wanting to deal with us in the same way today. We can all think back to times when we completely denied Jesus by the way that we lived and how we used to talk. Some of us may be having a tough time moving on from the past. You may be thinking to yourself…There was a time when I committed adultery, there was a time when I was hooked on pornography, there was a time when I was the biggest drinker around, there was a time in my business when I was the biggest crook of all. How can God use someone like that? But Jesus does not come to us today to make us feel guilty about our lack of commitment to Him in the past. He wants to restore us so that we will be useful and committed to Him now and into the future. You are never unusable to God because of your past. You are only unusable to God because of the attitude that you harbor about your past.

Think about the Apostle Paul's past. He killed Christians, and put them in prison. Yet God still had a great plan for this man with a checkered past. God doesn't want you to push your past under the rug and hide it deep down inside. He wants you to come to Him, broken about it, and He will remove it completely from you. He wants to reinstate you like He did Peter. He has great plans for you to help build up His kingdom.

Do Not Compare Your Service To Others

In verses 18-19, Jesus tells Peter, *"I tell you the truth, when you were younger you dressed yourself and went where you wanted; but when you are older you will stretch out your hands, and someone else will dress you and lead you where you do not want to go. Jesus said this to indicate the kind of death by which Peter would glorify God. Then he said to him, Follow me."* "Peter you are reinstated, pick up your cross and follow me." Jesus is saying, "Peter you're going to die for me." What was Peter's reaction to that? "What about him?" He was pointing at another disciple, and asking if he was going to have to die as well. It is so easy to get caught up and compare all that you are doing to what someone else is doing. "God, why have you called me to do all of this while so and so hardly does anything? Why should I volunteer to do something more when I already teach Sunday school, lead special music, and help with the youth group?" Or something I have heard, "I have put in my time, it is time for someone else to do it." Jesus never says that everyone will participate equally in His work. Unfortunately, a few people are saddled with most of the work in the church. We need to do what God has called us to do, and not worry about what others are or are not doing. Jesus wanted Peter to die for Him, He didn't ask the same of John. Your burden might be heavy, it may be heavier than someone else's, but carry it with joy because you know that your life is making a difference for God's kingdom.

Do not compare yourself to others. Be more intentional about the individual commitment that you have made to follow Jesus. Jesus said to Peter, "Do you love me more than these?" We don't know what Jesus meant by the word "these". Was Jesus talking about his boat, his nets, his fishing profession? Do you love me more than the money you can earn off of fishing? Just before this passage, Peter had just caught 153 fish. That is a big catch. After Peter denied Jesus, he went back and began to fish again. He went back to his old life.

I can see Jesus asking Peter, "Peter can you permanently leave your old life and follow me? Do you love me more than everything you see, more than any worldly thing or earthly relationship? If you do love me more than these, you will be able to take care of my sheep. But if you love other things more than you do me, then you will care more about yourself that you will about feeding my sheep. My sheep will suffer while you feed yourself." He is asking Peter, "Where do your loyalties lie? I want to know. I want to put you in charge of a great work, but I want to make sure that you don't use that position to feed yourself." I am heartbroken when I see pastors or Christian leaders living extravagant lives. Instead of denying themselves and modeling Christ's life to a fallen world, they feed off of their sheep. They use their sheep to make a lot of money and to gain more possessions for themselves. When we have been restored, our goal is to watch over one another.

Peter, after being reinstated, was willing to die for Jesus, something that he strayed away from earlier. You have to wonder how many people Peter influenced as he was willing to die for his faith. We know from history that many people came to the Lord as they saw a Christian standing strong in the faith as he was being killed.

> Back in the first century, Christians were not thought of too highly. In fact, many were condemned to die. One day, twelve men were condemned to die for being Christians. They were led by Roman soldiers out to a frozen pond. They were stripped of their clothes and made to stand on top of this frozen pond. They could have their clothes back and have a blanket thrown over them, if they would only renounce Christ. But the twelve stood at the middle of the pond for quite a long time shivering. They started to chant, "Twelve

men of God are we…Twelve men of God we will be." After a little while, it was too cold for one man, and he decided it wasn't worth it. He started back to the crowd and he was clothed with warm clothes and a blanket. But the chant continued. "Eleven men of God are we…Eleven men of God we will be." They said this over and over again, until there was a clanging noise on the ice. It was a Roman soldier taking off his gear, and clothes to go stand amongst the Christians. The chant continued, "Twelve men of God we are… twelve men of God we will be."[45]

I love that story. Our lives are a witness to a watching world. Have we been restored like Peter, and are we willing to die for our faith and be a witness to this lost world? God may ask you to sacrifice more than anyone else you know. Are you willing to follow through on what God has in store for your life? If you have encountered the Risen Christ, you should be ready to do anything for Him!

Conclusion

There is no doubt that this was the week that changed everything! Not much time passed from riding into Jerusalem on a donkey to carrying His cross to Golgotha, but the implications are tremendous. Not only did Jesus go from Humble King to Conquering King, but we went from enemies of God[46] to children of God.[47] Sin was done away with and now nothing can separate the faithful followers from their God. It was all because of this week that Jesus had had.

As we reflect on this week, and the implications that it has on our lives…never forget that God had it all planned. Nothing surprised Him. From the beginning of creation He knew the smallest details, down to which donkey Jesus would ride into Jerusalem. It is comforting to know that God knows what is going to happen in our lives and that He is in complete control. I never have to wonder if the mocking I receive or the harsh treatment that people give me or the physical abuse that comes to me is beyond His power to stop. I know that even His Son endured hardships on this earth. Maybe you are in the midst of a bad week right now. That is OK, because God can take the cross and bring new life out of it. It may take longer than three days for us to see the victory, but I know that God will bring us the victory.

The devil was defeated on Calvary. He still tries to play the game, but the final score has already been recorded. Jesus won, and we are all a part of His winning team. Don't fret if you feel like the devil is beating you right now; just don't quit. Jesus looked like He was up against the ropes on that faithful Friday afternoon, but by Sunday, there was no doubt who won the final victory. The devil, unfortunately, will win some battles once in a while in your life, but praise God that the end will reveal the true winners. The devil may win some battles, but through Jesus we have won the war!

Don't let the devil keep you out of the fight. He wants to keep you in your guilt and in your shame so that you will not be used by God to bring other people into His Kingdom. Let Jesus restore you. Catch a glimpse of the Risen Christ and receive the peace that He so desperately wants to give you. Find your fulfillment in serving your King!

The King has come, He sacrificed Himself for you, and He rose to conquer death once and for all. Now it is up to you to respond. The Risen King holds out His arms to welcome you as His child. You can continue with your life like this week didn't happen, or you can embrace the gift of God and surrender your life to Him. But as for me, this week changed my life! I am a child of the King!

If you believe that this week changed your life, please pray the following prayer with me.

Lord Jesus,
We worship You that You left the perfect place of heaven to live among us. Not only did

You leave heaven, but You endured the pain and shame that we deserved. Thank You for not quitting halfway through the week. You loved us enough to take the suffering and the cross that was meant for us. We marvel at the sacrifice that You made to save sinners like us. We want to live committed lives to our Risen King. We long to spend eternity with the King who conquered death on our behalf. We love You and praise You. In Jesus' precious name we pray, AMEN.

ENDNOTES

[1] Matthew 26:53
[2] Luke 9:58
[3] 1 Corinthians 15:26
[4] *"To Whom Shall I Leave My Kingdom?"*, Donald E. Wildmon. More Stories for the Heart, Compiled by Alice Gray, (Multnomah Publishers, 1997). p. 88.
[5] Luke 9:58
[6] Isaiah 53:2
[7] *"Playing with Anticipation"*, 1002 Humorous Illustrations for Public Speaking, Michael E. Hodgin, p. 390.
[8] Luke 21:1-4
[9] *"Worshipping or Accusing"*, Illustrations on Logos Bible Software.
[10] 2 Samuel 6: 14-22
[11] *Forfeiting the Opportunity of a Lifetime"*, Reuters News Service (8-19-03); submitted by Greg Asimakoupoulos, Naperville, Illinois. (Preachingtoday.com)
[12] Matthew 7:21-23
[13] Matthew 7:13-14
[14] *"No Burglar-Proof Glass"*, "Illustrations from Logos Software.
[15] Cannot locate source.
[16] Charles R. Swindoll, *Living Above the Level of Mediocrity.* Swindoll's Ultimate Book of Illustrations & Quotes, Charles R. Swindoll, Thomas Nelson Publishers, 1998.
[17] *"Communion Snack"* Elizabeth Charles Gomes, Wyncote, Penn., Today's Christian Woman, "Heart to Heart." (preachingtoday.com)
[18] *"Christ the Instructing One-Abiding"*, Dr. James McCullen. http://www.preachhim.org//john15.htm.htm
[19] Malachi 3:10
[20] *"Humor: United Divided Church."* Cartoonist Ed Koehler, Leadership, Vol. 8, no. 4. (Preachingtoday.com)
[21] *"Misunderstood Children's Sermon"* Marilyn McCoy, Chester, Vermont. Christian Reader, "Kids of the Kingdom." (Preachingtoday.com)
[22] "Attacking Others, Hurting Jesus" Lee Rhodes, Wheeler, Michigan (Preachingtoday.com)
[23] *"A Guy Named Bill"*, Rebecca Manley Pippert. More Stories for the Heart, Compiled by Alice Gray, Multnomah Publishers, 1997.
[24] *"The Myth of the Lighthouse"*, Paul Aiello, Jr., Leadership, Vol. 4, no. 2. (Preachingtoday.com)
[25] John 10:18

[26] *"Debunking Pluralism"*, Timothy Keller, "Preaching Amid Pluralism," Leadership Journal (Winter 2002, vol. XXIV, no. 1), p. 34. (preachingtoday.com)
[27] John Hess-Yoder, Portland, Oregon, Leadership, Vol. 7, no. 3. (Preachingtoday.com)
[28] *"Hope after Crucifixion"* William D. Barrick, Christian Reader, Vol. 35, no. 2 (Preachingtoday.com)
[29] *"God's Son Punished for our Sin."* Bryan Chapell, The Wonder of it All (Crossway, 1999); quoted in Men of Integrity (March/April 2001) (Preachingtoday.com)
[30] *"Jesus Our Stunt Double"* Joel Saurault in Fresh Illustration for Preaching & Teaching (Baker), from the editors of Leadership. (Preachingtoday.com)
[31] *"Grieving Father Trusts Eternal Shipbuilder"*, Richard Exley, "Decent Exposure", Leadership (Fall 1992) p. 118. (Preachingtoday.com)
[32] Cannot locate source.
[33] *"FBI Agent Denied Pizza Delivery"*, Kevin A. Miller, vice president, Christianity Today International; source: www.vasthumor.isfunny.com; and www.snopes.com (Preachingtoday.com)
[34] Carolyn Arends, "What's So Good About Good Friday?" Kyria.com (4-10-09) Preachingtoday.com
[35] *"An Odd and Challenging Resurrection"*, Wolfhart Pennenberg, in a conversation with Prism magazine. (Preachingtoday.com)
[36] *"Yet I Will Praise Him."* Vernon Grounds, Denver, Colorado. Leadership, Vol. 8, no. 1. (Preachingtoday.com)
[37] Gangel, Kenneth. Holman New Testament Commentary, Broadman & Holman Publishers, 2000, page 365.
[38] Based on *"Phantom Guilt"* Dr Paul Brand and Philip Yancey, Leadership, Vol. 5, no. 3. (Preachingtoday.com)
[39] *"Blind to What's in Front of You"* John Ross, Surrey, England, Leadership, Vol. 8, no. 4. (Preachingtoday.com)
[40] Cannot locate source.
[41] *"Epigram on Doubters"*, Illustrations on Logos Bible System.
[42] *"Faith is the Unseen"*, Vesper Bauer, Audubon, Iowa, Christian Reader (Sept/Oct 1998). (Preachingtoday.com)
[43] *"The Day Philip Joined the Group"*, Paul Harvey. Stories of the Heart, Compiled by Alice Gray, Questar Publishers, 1996.
[44] *"Jesus the Explorer"* D. James Kennedy, "Message from an Empty Tomb," Preaching Today, Tape No. 66.
[45] Cannot locate source.
[46] Colossians 1:21-22
[47] John 1:12

Need additional copies?

To order more copies of
Humble King To Conquering King,
contact NewBookPublishing.com

- ❏ Order online at NewBookPublishing.com
- ❏ Call 877-311-5100 or
- ❏ Email Info@NewBookPublishing.com

Call for multiple copy discounts!

Reliance Media

Additional Books by Kurt Litwiller

*Living Out
The
Called Life*
Running God's Race

New Covenant Living
**Released to
Live by the Spirit**

*Changed by the
King's
Presence*

Order Your Copies Today!